CW01272820

REINVENTING DEMOCRACY

IMPROVING BRITISH POLITICAL GOVERNANCE

The right of David Kauders to be identified as the author of this work has been asserted under the terms of the Copyright, Designs and Patents Act, 1988.

Nothing in this book constitutes a financial promotion for the purposes of Section 21 of the Financial Services and Markets Act 2000 (UK), nor is anything in this book to be construed as financial advice for the purposes of the Investment Advisers Act of 1940 (USA).
No warranty is given with regard to the accuracy or completeness of any information herein. The author and publisher disclaim any liability or responsibility for any loss arising directly or indirectly from the use of any material in this book.

Without limiting the rights under copyright reserved herein, no part of this publication may be reproduced, stored in or introduced into a retrieval system or transmitted by any form or by any means without the prior written permission of the publisher. Except in the United States of America, this publication may not be hired out, whether for a fee or otherwise, in any cover or binding other than as supplied by the publisher.

Every effort has been made to trace copyright holders and to obtain permission for the use of copyrighted material. The publisher apologises for any errors or omissions and would be grateful if notified of any corrections that should be incorporated in future reprints or editions of this book. A catalogue record for this book is available from the British Library.

All rights reserved.

2.0

First published in 2024 by Sparkling Books Limited

Copyright © David Kauders 2024

ISBN: 9781907230202

E-book: 9781907230226

TABLE OF CONTENTS

PREFACE	**15**
SUMMARY OF PRINCIPAL CONCEPTS	**19**
1 A COUNTRY THAT HAS LOST ITS WAY	**21**
Uncomfortable truths	24
Britain and Europe	28
What rights do you have?	29
What does the future hold?	31
2 MAJOR UK POLICY FAILURES	**32**
The seven major mistakes	32
The cumulative effect of policy failures	37
Measures of living standards	37
Privatisation	39
The UK retail energy market	*39*
Water	*40*
Rail	*43*
3 THE CASE FOR CONSTITUTIONAL CHANGE	**45**
What makes a society successful?	45

The dead-end of political evolution	46
The road to British serfdom	*49*
Other failures	53
Closing ranks against the truth	54
The democratic deficit	56
Federal systems of governance	57
Borders	66
Direct democracy	67
Broader economic issues	*68*
Overseas territories	69
Linking the issues	71

4 OUTLINE OF A SOLUTION — 73

Learning from the gross mistake	76
Sovereignty	77
Compete, compromise, cooperate, and consult	79
The numerical dominance of England	83
Central or local? Who pays the piper?	84
International agreements	86
Artificial intelligence and the tech industries	86
What else?	87

5 THE PEOPLE'S COUNCIL — 88

Functions of the People's Council	88
Organisations forming the British State	*90*
Truthfulness and standards	*91*
Requests for referenda	*93*
Listening to the people	*93*
Assent to legislation	*94*
Ombudspersons	*94*
The facts hub	*94*

    Referrals to the Constitutional Court   95
  Legislative mandates and venues   95
    The people's assent   96
  Choosing and refreshing the People's Council   97
    1. The regulated group   99
    2. The general group   99
    3. The sortition group   100
    Leadership, building expertise, teamwork   100

6 THE NEW GOVERNMENTS   103

  Levels of governance and oversight   103
    UK responsibilities   103
    England, Scotland, Wales, Northern Ireland, and overseas territories   106
    Regions   106
  The need for change   106
  Revenue and borrowing   107
    UK government revenue   108
    Revenues of England, Scotland, Wales, and Northern Ireland   108
    Revenue sources for the regions   108
    Government borrowing   108
    User fees   110
    Wealth taxes   110
  Pensions, healthcare costs, and social security   110
  Other changes that are needed   111

7 HOW CHANGE COULD BE ACHIEVED   114

    England   116
    Scotland and Wales   117
    Northern Ireland   117
  Interpretation of preliminary results   117

Adopting the new constitution	119
Timeline	120

8 FIRST-DRAFT CONSTITUTION OF THE UNITED KINGDOM 121

Notes	121
The draft Constitution	121
Overseas Territories of the United Kingdom	130
Citizens	130
The State and the citizen	136
The law	138
Social objectives	144
Relations between the arms of government, financial equalisation, and legal relations	144
Foreign affairs	148
Military, security, police, and emergency services	149
Culture, education, and religion	150
Infrastructure and essential services	151
Government accounts, the national debt, and taxation	156
Healthcare	158
Business, the economy, common regulation, and standards	159
Pensions and benefits	162
Elections to parliaments and local authorities	163
Legislation	168
Ombudspersons	170
The People's Council	171
Membership of the People's Council	181
Honours	187
Entry into force	188
Changes to this Constitution	189
Further transitional provisions	191
The Constitutional Court	193

APPENDIX A: THE PRIVATE FINANCE INITIATIVE (PFI)	**194**
APPENDIX B: RIGHTS	**202**
REFERENCES	**205**
INDEX	**218**
SPARKLING BOOKS	**243**

TABLES

1.	Falling living standards in the UK	38
2.	Derivative liabilities and assets at Thames Water	41
3.	Comparisons of federal and devolved states	59
4.	Further comparisons of federal and devolved states	59
5.	Non-native languages in the UK	63
6.	Effect of proposed private finance initiative at Edinburgh Royal Infirmary (2002)	196
7.	PFI costs at Durham hospital (2002)	197

FIGURES

1.	Example of a multi-choice referendum	77
2.	The People's Council	101
3.	Governments, if England adopts regions	104
4.	Governments, if England rejects regions	105

ABOUT THE AUTHOR

David Kauders FRSA was educated at Latymer Upper School, Jesus College Cambridge, and Cranfield School of Management. He is an investment manager and author.

BY THE SAME AUTHOR

The Greatest Crash: Avoiding the financial system limit (revised edition 2024)

Understanding Brexit Options: What future for Britain?

The Financial System Limit: The world's real debt burden (UK edition, hard cover, subtitle: Britain's real debt burden, includes UK postscript)

Bear Markets: When finance turns upside down (forthcoming)

ACKNOWLEDGEMENTS

This book evolved in stages, with various contributors helping as it progressed. Michael Meadowcroft read an early draft and observed that despite much analysis, nobody had previously succeeded in changing our political system. Four contributors wish to remain anonymous for different reasons; one did much of the early work on the People's Council and the responsibilities of governments; two researched Wikepedia. Dan Amery gave me a point of view from a younger generation. Tom Brake read a much later draft and gave me useful ideas about representation in the People's Council. Georgina Weaver edited the book, Larch Gallagher designed the book and cover, and Sharon Laverick indexed the print edition.

This book is dedicated to

Anna

in recognition of her encouragement and endless patience

"Paint over Mickey Mouse
Burn Where the Wild Things Are
Pulverise the Lego
Set fire to the Christmas tree star.

Seize all the teddies.
Bury every skipping rope
Paint the walls dark brown
Abolish all hope."

– Michael Rosen,
Children's Author, 9 July 2023

PREFACE

The British public have low confidence in their political system:

Confidence in	
Government	24%
Parliament	22%
Political parties	13%
The press	13%

This disturbing academic research was published by the policy institute at King's College London in March 2023[1].

Three months later, a Focaldata survey for the Institute for Public Policy Research[2], looking at the entire political system, found that:

90% think the system needs reform
(with gradations of completely, to a large extent, and to some extent)
6% are satisfied with the current system, and
4% do not know.

This book argues that the British system of political governance has evolved to a dead-end. Only by accepting this position can we hope to find a way out of the morass, exemplified by rising poverty levels and declining public services that are unlikely to be solved by a change of government. This failure of political governance has obvious economic and social consequences.

The argument in this book is short and blunt. In my view, British politics are unable to promote compromise and suffer frequent short-term changes of direction. The people have no right to put anything on the policy agenda; instead, they are fed lies, spin, and disinformation. According to Peter Oborne, Britain is ruled by a corrupt political and financial elite[3].

There has been an appalling succession of scandals, showing that the British State is out of control[4]. Other countries also have scandals, but British ones seem to affect many people at the same time. Politicians only respond to public concerns when a general election is due. Immediate pressures then force deeper issues to one side. This book attempts to redress the balance between the immediate issues and the more complex, deeper ones that are rarely considered.

If the United Kingdom (UK) is to improve its democracy, it needs a clear vision of what it is aiming to achieve and the steps towards that objective. Vested interests will always raise objections. Yet this statement by the Institute for Public Policy and Research says it all:

> "No matter who's in power, our democratic machine needs rewiring. If people are once again to be authors of their own lives, and to feel secure, they must sense their influence in the collective decision-making endeavour that is democracy"[5].

Your author is British, now living in a European democracy. From a distance, the author has perhaps found it easier to see some of the faults in British governance and its political economy than may be apparent to those entombed within a system stuck in the past, closing ranks against new ideas, fixing only immediate problems that threaten the governing party.

This book will suggest scope for improvement for the benefit of the people – the people who are largely ignored, sometimes trampled upon. Democracy should be power to the people against the elites. The fundamental problem is that the British State gives absolute power to a select few. You, reader, may not agree with everything in this book. My purpose is to stimulate discussion, not prescribe a complete answer. Britain desperately needs a written constitution for a federal state, in which decisions are taken at the most sensible level, and what follows can only be a starting point to chart a route for the future. This would reinvigorate politics at all levels, keeping decision-makers in touch with us all.

While this book is primarily about and for the UK, some of the concepts could be adapted by other countries also concerned about sliding into autocracy. The mother of parliaments exported representative parliamentary democracy to the free world, but also provided the model of two gladiators fighting for absolute power. Now it has the chance to lead the world in updating its democracy for the twenty-first century and beyond.

Many other books have been written about the state of British political governance. Gavin Esler, in *Britain is Better than This*, sets out a much more detailed explanation of the failure of British political governance[6]. Mark E Thomas covers mass impoverishment in far more detail than my short explanation of repeated policy failures, in his book *99%: How We've Been Screwed and How to Fight Back*. His case is that 99% of the British population have falling living standards because the rewards have gone to a select few[7]. Rory Stewart shows how members of parliament in the governing party are nothing more than tools of the current elected dictator[8]. This author accepts all these analyses.

There is one factor missing from every book and think tank paper that I have seen. Nobody else has put forward a draft written constitution for the British people to consider. In this sense, this book is unique.

PREFACE

My proposals for a federal structure with a written constitution and a People's Council will be seen by some as too much change for a country liking the way things have always been done. It would amount to replacing centralised by dispersed power. There are two problems with eschewing these principles:

1. Nothing – or very little – would change, the scandals would repeat with new names but the same mistakes, people would be downtrodden, and economic decline would continue.
2. The concepts in this book are interlinked. Some details can indeed be altered, and the people should be able to vote on them. But this is not a menu to select from, rather an integrated whole that attempts to move Britain out of its seventeenth century model of two tribes fighting for the right to be absolute despots.

Britain needs to grasp the whole problem of its political governance.
David Kauders
(a founder member of Kauders Portfolio Management AG)
Zug, Switzerland, February 2024

SUMMARY OF PRINCIPAL CONCEPTS

1. The House of Lords and Privy Council should both be replaced by a directly elected apolitical People's Council, according to a written, comprehensible, constitution that encourages consensus, and has clear objectives.

2. Sovereignty should be redefined as sovereignty of the people of each of the nations of the UK, instead of the Crown in Parliament.

3. The UK should be a federal association with dispersed, not central, power. The UK parliament could mainly be responsible for defence, foreign affairs, the currency, trade, and common standards.

4. There should be an associate status for overseas territories that are independent, save for reliance on Britain for their defence, foreign representation, and legal appeals. All overseas territories should have representation in the UK parliament and the rights to fully integrate with the UK or leave the UK completely.

5. Near-absolute central power should be replaced by dispersed power. Appropriate part-time involvement in political governance could be possible at many levels, provided there is no conflict of

interest. The absolute power of governments based on the divine right of Kings should be ended.

6. Any UK referendum should require a majority of the nations to vote in favour in addition to a majority of the votes cast. Whether to hold national and local referenda is a matter for the sovereign nations. England should not be able to use its numeric superiority to impose its will on the other nations.

7. There should be two-way transfer funding at government level to financially support nations and regions.

8. Although a written constitution could be adopted for a unitary State, only a federal structure would prevent the UK from breaking up.

9. There should be proper controls over political, government, and media communications, including lobbying. All communications should be clear, fair, and not misleading.

10. At present, Britons are serfs to a powerful State. With this draft Constitution they would be citizens with rights and, hopefully, pride in the country.

1 A COUNTRY THAT HAS LOST ITS WAY

There is a pervading sense that, in Britain, nothing works as it should. Many individual policy failures have brought about near-Victorian conditions, with rising child poverty[9], deteriorating healthcare, insanitary housing, even reports of people using pliers to pull out their own teeth. Left unchecked, these Victorian conditions may well recreate some relics of the Middle Ages. They arise from an unending series of errors. This book will show how the system of political governance can be improved, to reduce future errors.

British politics are built around two tribes fighting one another, straight out of the English civil war. The gladiators leading the tribes manoeuvre using national media, creating traps for the other side, name-calling like schoolboys, and sowing division. They do little to educate or lead the public, and rarely promote consensus. Power games are more important to our politicians than 'doing the right thing', as evidenced by the 2023 retreat from climate change targets together with extension of North Sea oil and gas licensing[10].

British politicians exploit diversionary exercises on a grand scale: for example, austerity, Europe, devolution, and asylum seekers. Ideas have been proposed for amending the British constitution[11], but nobody has made the case for complete replacement and offered a comprehensive solution. This book attempts both.

Two items that appeared in June 2023 made the extent of British decline clear. The first was an opinion article[12] by Dr Adam Posen, an American economist who served on the Bank of England's monetary policy committee from 2009 to 2012. He argued that it is time for the UK to think like an emerging market. But emerging markets are usually developing countries that are improving their lot; to this author, Britain seems to be going the other way. Two days later, the King's Fund published a report on health outcomes, which showed that the UK is a laggard on these outcomes as regards both treatment and survivability, which is linked to fewer resources (e.g. hospital beds, scanners) and poorer staffing levels than those of other countries[13].

Brexit has brought the failure of the British system of political governance to a head. Enough people believed sufficient lies to create an economic, social, and diplomatic mistake. Britain's governance is prone to extremist capture and utterly short-term in its thinking. We let them make a mess then throw the rascals out. Better not to make such a mess in the first place.

Brexit has served to illuminate the damage caused by an unstable winner-take-all political and governance system that is incapable of coping with the complex world of the twenty-first century. Timid policies, incremental changes, and muddling through with piecemeal reforms will fail. Even worse, Britain is slowly discovering that it has no economic choice but to follow European Union (EU) rules that it can no longer make or influence, which turns the UK into a powerless vassal state.

On a scale of 100% democracy to 100% autocracy, Britain must rank as one of the least democratic countries, an autocratic country excepting an occasional change in the ruling elite. The key element of British democracy is that two parties compete for absolute power: two autocrats take turns at imposing their world view. The first-past-the-post electoral system prevents other parties from competing, which would surely be a breach of competition law if that law applied to politics as regards monopolies and duopolies. Differences compared to North Korea are a matter of degree (isolation, falling living standards, dislike of foreigners, loss of rights, and restricted travel are common to both countries) although North Korea is many decades behind the UK in terms of living standards. The reason Britain is so undemocratic is that the supposedly flexible unwritten British constitution slowly removes power from the people and hands it to the elite. Governments with control of the Commons can pass any legislation they like. When they legislate to fix a constitutional problem only two situations can result:

1. The fix becomes a nuisance after a time, in which case they legislate again to overturn it. Hence fixed-term parliaments, to bind the 2010 coalition together, overturned by the 2019 government. Likewise, the 2011 law to prevent transfer of more power to the EU, overturned when it obstructed the arrangements for leaving. Both of these examples originated during the Conservative and Liberal Democrat coalition and were reversed by later Conservative governments.

2. The fix reduces democratic accountability, in which case it becomes permanent and not open to challenge. Lloyd George stripped the Lords of power to block the Commons indefinitely, and even Gordon Brown did not dare to propose restoring such power to his intended assembly of the nations and regions.

Britain is not alone. The West faces a collective problem of rising autocracy. China is slowly forming a grouping of autocratic client states. Russia is now a Chinese client state, dependent on sales of oil and gas, through a new pipeline (not yet complete), to offset Western sanctions. India and South Africa chose not to condemn the Russian invasion of Ukraine and have participated in naval exercises with China. Iran and

Saudi Arabia, long bitter opponents in the Shia-Sunni divide, restored diplomatic relations following Chinese intervention. The future world order will be autocratic states led by China, versus democratic states. If a future American president loses interest in the world of free democratic nations, who will lead the democracies?

In his book *The Crisis of Democratic Capitalism*[14], Martin Wolf argues that democratic countries perform better economically than autocratic countries. It follows that Britain's poor economic performance can be linked to its inadequate democracy. I will present some evidence of the decline in living standards in Chapter 2.

UNCOMFORTABLE TRUTHS

If we ask ourselves, 'What is Britain's place in the world?' then some uncomfortable truths emerge:

1. Britain tries to punch above its weight internationally, but lacks the military means to do so. The people show little enthusiasm for waging *offensive* military action.

2. Britain's influence on the world stage has been damaged by Brexit. The government behaves as if it remembers nothing from 47 years of EU membership and sometimes forgets that it has signed a trade and cooperation agreement with the EU[15].

3. Britain uses gross domestic product (GDP) statistics to convince itself that it is an economic power, ignoring the inequalities of income and scale of household debt on which this conviction is based.

4. Britain pretends to be a bastion of freedom, even though Britons have few rights and little privacy.

5. Britons delude themselves that they are the fount of modern democracy, despite electing governments on a minority of votes,

with scant popular support expressed through the ballot box. The oldest democracy is now an obsolete model, long overdue for replacement.

There are some uncomfortable truths about the working of government. Ministers are appointed who have little or no expertise in the departments they supposedly direct. There are no subject expertise or qualification requirements. Instead, there is a merry-go-round from which ministers move on to new posts frequently. Amateurs are inappropriate to the complex world of the twenty-first century.

We will see later how the British people have been financially exploited by various methods of financial engineering. This is symptomatic of the attitude that the people are serfs, to a State that does not serve them. Perhaps the government should, instead, be the servant of the people?

Autocratic government and financial exploitation may be why the economy performs poorly. Economists have long puzzled over the lower productivity gains achieved by Britain vis-a-vis other European countries. The failures brought about by British political governance are, I believe, a consequence of the lack of a written constitution. As Conan Doyle wrote in *The Sign of the Four*, "When you have eliminated the impossible, whatever remains, however improbable, must be the truth."

The dot.com bust at the beginning of the millennium was the predictable result of excess credit driving investment in the 'new economy'. Businesses over-expanded and duly collapsed, taking the small investor's savings down in the process.

The financial crisis of 2007 to 2009 was different. Its proximate cause was banks withdrawing from wholesale financial markets as derivative losses spread from American property. The consequence was a severe global recession driven by lack of bank lending.

By 2009, the British people were furious about banks creating dangerous products that blew up, resulting in the credit crunch. That fury was misplaced, because banks could never have created the dangerous derivatives if governments had kept the credit supply under control. Now we have a crisis of democracy. Another recession is brewing and will unleash a new wave of disaffection with politicians.

The global way out from the dot.com and credit crunch disasters was to repeat the credit expansion trick, thereby creating the next downturn, which is now arriving via inflation, mortgage distress, reduced bank lending, and recession. Fighting inflation with higher interest rates has been fashionable, but half a century ago inflation was fought by withdrawing credit from the banking system. There was no need to push people into debt poverty; the old method could have been resurrected.

When banks choose or are forced to reduce their lending, the capacity of businesses and households to service and repay existing debts also shrinks, with declining asset prices. The current path to recession is new, because there is no one definite start point. It is rolling around the world, bringing political upsets and territorial disputes in its wake. China is heading into deflation: falling prices and economic shrinkage. The second largest economy may yet export deflation to the world.

Political upsets are a direct consequence of insufficient growth, or, in some cases, continued economic sclerosis. These political upsets include:

- population displacement as a result of war, famine, disease, and climate change
- the rise of disruptive extremists on the right, such as the Freedom Caucus and Trump in America, the Reform Party in Britain, the National Rally in France, and Jobbik in Hungary

- the appearance of disruptive elements on the left, such as Syriza in Greece, and the Scottish National Party (SNP) in Britain, although they have all been neutered for now
- the attack on immigrants and refugees, both across Europe and particularly in Britain.

There are two other points about the economy that have contributed to decline:

1. mistaken understanding of free trade, and
2. financial engineering.

In *The Wealth of Nations*, Adam Smith wrote,

> "People of the same trade seldom meet together, even for merriment and diversion, but the conversation ends in a conspiracy against the public, or in some contrivance to raise prices."

His message was that markets should be free of conspiracies against the public. By constantly using the expression 'free markets', some politicians have transformed Smith's insight into the exact opposite, that businesses must be allowed to do as they choose. This has constrained effective regulation in Britain.

Financial engineering has been used to extract money from the British economy, thereby depressing incomes and raising household costs. We shall see how this was carried out in the case studies in Chapter 2 and Appendix A.

BRITAIN AND EUROPE

Britain has always had an uneasy relationship with Europe. For most of the seventeenth, eighteenth, and nineteenth centuries, Britain tried to prevent a strong power from emerging on the European continent. The need for this policy was reinforced by the emergence of Germany as a major power in the 1870s and then by subsequent wars.

EU membership required compromises with other neighbouring countries in the collective interest, for those matters that were EU competences. The world has become more complex, even in my lifetime, and nearly half a century of membership disguised some of the shortcomings of the British constitution. Now, outside the EU, those shortcomings are more obvious.

Slowly, Britain is discovering that it benefited greatly from EU membership, and many opinion polls report that a majority now believe it was wrong to leave. This shows that lies and disinformation need to be expunged from the body politic. **Given accurate facts and effective mechanisms to stop political lies, the people can be trusted to make better decisions than politicians.** This book will only say little about the EU, but it is axiomatic that Britain will need to handle two major changes at the same time:

1. getting much closer to Europe, whether via intermediate steps through the single market and customs union, or directly by trying to rejoin the EU (so as to make the rules once more), and
2. repairing its serious democratic deficit.

This book is concerned with the second major change. If politicians continue to deny the reality about Europe, then at least reforming the political system will allow the people to place Europe on the agenda. The democratic deficit means that Britain must choose between a major reform to enhance democracy, or sliding into complete autocracy as the elites exploit the 'flexible' constitution to continue stripping the British people of their rights.

WHAT RIGHTS DO YOU HAVE?

The 2019 British government intended to replace the Human Rights Act, which incorporates the European Convention on Human Rights (ECHR) with a British bill of rights but has now abandoned that exercise. There is frequent talk of leaving the European Convention, thereby joining Belarus and Russia as pariah states. Britain was a leading player in creating the ECHR in 1950, which itself implements the Universal Declaration of Human Rights of 1948.

Although British rights are often traced back to Magna Carta (1215), they originated with the Assize of Clarendon in 1186, under Henry II, which led to the abolition of trial by combat and trial by ordeal, and the development of the English (and later, Scottish) jury system.

Rights do not depend on citizenship: they apply to everyone[16]. I include a full explanation of rights in Appendix B.

Up against the State, which has unlimited resources and denies you legal aid, here are some ways in which the right to a fair trial is undermined:

1. 'Fast track' extradition treaties, in which evidence is not tested in a British court.

2. Civil penalties such as anti-social behaviour orders being used to avoid criminal proceedings. These rely on 'the balance of probabilities' rather than the more stringent test of 'beyond reasonable doubt'.

3. Closed courts and secret evidence, notably control orders, family court restrictions, detention without trial, extraordinary rendition,

and the partially secret court known as the Special Immigration Appeals Commission.

4. The Justice and Security Act 2013, which overturned the principle that nobody is above the law, introducing the Orwellian trial by 'closed material proceedings'. The Equality and Human Rights Commission (EHRC) gave evidence to the House of Lords that closed material proceedings would be incompatible with the right to a fair trial. Three members of the Commission resigned in protest at the government forcing the law through.

To the extent that the right to privacy is a legal right recognised in the UK, it arises from a patchwork of laws and cases, the latter often resulting from celebrity or media issues. It is undermined by state databases and surveillance powers. Local authorities can use surveillance without judicial oversight. Automatic number plate recognition is now used widely on Britain's roads, with no restrictions. Police forces are being given access to all images in the driving licence database[17]. CCTV use depends only on a code of conduct. Criminal record checks may reveal unsubstantiated allegations to potential employers. Britain has one of the largest per capita DNA databases in the world, collected forcibly from every arrest even where no charge or conviction follows. Some restrictions on this were introduced in 2013, notably in cases where no charge was laid, or a person was acquitted.

The 2019 Conservative general election manifesto promised to

"... raise standards in workers' and environmental rights ... high standards with a balance of rights and entitlements ... Judicial review would protect the rights of the individual against an overbearing state ... We will continue to champion human rights",

but subsequent policies have been somewhat different. Voting rights, demonstration rights, and free-movement rights have already been curtailed[18]. It would be more accurate to describe Britons as subjects, subjects of an autocratic executive.

As for the disrespect that some government agencies have for the citizen, I refer you to an article[19] by the author, Jamal Osman, who is of Somali origin, naturalised British, and is a successful journalist. Under the title 'I am a British citizen, not a second class citizen', he described how the border force treated him every time he arrived at Heathrow from a foreign news assignment. What he described could possibly be the product of the surveillance state amplified by discrimination. Rights are fine in theory, but in practice they may be treated with contempt.

WHAT DOES THE FUTURE HOLD?

Forecasting longer-term trends is notoriously difficult. However, there are two areas with which the UK political system will struggle to cope without major reform. They are climate change and the weight of private sector debt. Politicians talk about net zero without considering whether this may be an inadequate target. They also talk about government debt, without mentioning the far greater business and household debt levels that they and their predecessors have encouraged through past stimulus policies. Britain needs to face up to both.

Two other areas are ignored in contemporary discourse. One is that the young need a future. Governance has become too biased towards the older generations. This is why my ideas include scope for part-time involvement and career steps for the younger generations.

My other concern is that pro-Europeans still share the imperial delusion with leavers, that Britain can get what it wants when it chooses. Getting closer to Europe may be painful. Many countries are fed up with Britain and its incoherent demands for special treatment. Only standard solutions are likely to be on offer. But rejoining may not be easy. De Gaulle vetoed the original application in 1960. An existing member could exercise its veto.

2 MAJOR UK POLICY FAILURES

THE SEVEN MAJOR MISTAKES

The UK's system of political governance has failed. This is the truth revealed by Brexit, but it is only one of a series of major failures. There have been seven major policy failures in the last forty years:

1. some infrastructure privatisations
2. the private finance initiative (PFI)
3. the influence of the oligarch class
4. political lies
5. austerity
6. the Brexit referendum
7. taxation policy

The process started with the idealism of privatisation, ending the mixed economy that had prevailed between 1945 and 1982. Some of the privatisations initially improved competition and standards, notably in telecommunications. On the other hand, infrastructure privatisation was not always so successful. Water privatisation has turned into a scandal of low investment, filthy rivers and beaches, high wastage, and excessive prices caused by rent extraction (i.e. owners taking excessive rewards by more than one method, an example of the broad subject of financial engineering). England is among the few countries in the world with privatised water and drainage.

It is claimed that railway privatisation has resulted in British travellers subsidising those European travellers whose state railways have acquired British operators. We will examine this claim in depth later in this chapter.

The private finance initiative (PFI) saddled Britons with excessive debt service costs and service reductions to meet those costs. Because it involved thirty-year contracts, this overhang will continue for another decade. Early experiments were carried out by the Conservative government under John Major, but the majority of the debt was incurred by the Blair Labour government.

The influence of the oligarch class emerged slowly with neo-liberalism. The journalist George Monbiot has a description of the oligarch class on YouTube[20]. Oligarchs may play in Britain without contributing fully to society. Britain does not raise enough in taxes to properly fund public services because its tax base is rather narrow. UK residence and domicile rules leave many loopholes for those with multiple homes to stay in Britain without paying taxes. A simple, fair system would tax anyone who stays more than six months in a year, even in several parts, on their worldwide income and assets. One of the points made by Dr. Posen in the *Financial Times*[12] was that Britain needs higher taxes on the wealthy to properly fund healthcare and infrastructure.

Political lies have become a major problem. The decline in standards started with claims about Iraqi weapons of mass destruction, then was extended by **austerity**, which cut public services that the poor depend on, cut funding to local government and the justice and prisons system, yet maintained tax favours for others[21].

The present governing party has a love affair with austerity, in the belief that the books can be balanced by squeezing the poor mercilessly. Austerity was sold as good for the nation, but it only benefited the better-off, those who make less use of public services. Instead, austerity has been a contributing factor in damaging public services. Research by the Rowntree Foundation showed that people in deprived areas believed that leaving the EU would put an end to austerity[22]. The politicians who sold this to the people were misleading them. They continue to mislead, offering tax cuts now to be paid for later, hopefully – to those misleading you – under a different government.

The British public have long believed that 20% to 40% of welfare claimants are scroungers, but the true figure for benefit fraud was 0.7% a decade ago[23]; it has risen slightly following the pandemic[24]. The real problem here is that almost nobody in government, the economics and finance professions, or national media, has any experience of abject poverty. The poorest families in the UK have endured a frightening collapse in living standards[25]. Benefits are meagre compared to those in other European countries.

That 2016 referendum was a disgrace. Almost every promise made was a lie. For a long time, I thought that the crucial lie was "They need us more than we need them", which was based on a complete misconception of trade statistics, as if they related to the UK in relation to one other country, not the UK versus twenty-seven others[26]. However, I have changed my view. The crucial lie was "Brussels rules" because British politicians hid behind the EU when they wanted to impose unpopular policies. Britain was on the winning side in over 85% of European Council decisions[27]. When you have to pay for the new Schengen travel permits, remember that the system was originally designed by the UK when it was an EU member. EU changes take time because they are widely considered by member states and the European parliament. British changes are forced through its parliament by governments determined to show results quickly, using control of business in the House of Commons, routine adoption of timetable motions, and the implied threat of career damage if their MPs do not vote as instructed by the party whips.

Why was almost everything a lie? Perhaps it was related to the EU tax transparency directive[28], which was hated by the oligarch class. Was this why a handful of oligarchs found a legal way to fund a second Leave campaign? And the misrepresentations continue. In a BBC *Question Time* programme in early 2023, a political editor claimed that the UK had to leave the single market in order to strike its own trade deals. Did the contributor hope that participants and viewers would not know the difference between the single market and the customs union[29]? Was it a simple mistake? Why was it not corrected on air? It took place in the first fifteen minutes of a much longer programme, giving ample time for a correction. Since then, the UK has arrived at a worse trade agreement with Canada, because it lacks the clout of the vast European market.

Meanwhile, nothing gets done about a wide agenda of inadequate policies, because trivial point-scoring in the media is more attractive than deep thought about policy. Simon Jenkins identified the shallowness of bipartisan debate and the loss of forward-looking Royal Commissions as major factors, listing the NHS, falling life expectancy, water, energy, the school curriculum, asylum and immigration policies, drug misuse, food additives, housing, and prison overcrowding among the areas of neglect. Nothing happens. Nobody has a clue what to do. Of true reform there is no sign[30]. He could have added (but did not) household debt, poverty, food banks, declining inward investment, woeful trade agreements, and the maintenance backlog in schools and hospitals (worsened by the concrete crisis)[31]. This is the measure of a failing state.

British politics are unstable, and it is my view that this instability damages economic growth. The people were not asked what sort of Brexit they wanted; the centrist options of the single market, with or without the customs union, were never offered.

By contrast, compromise is integral in other European democracies. In Switzerland, the federal cabinet (called the Federal Council) is a permanent coalition of the parties, whereby each party has one or two cabinet places and elects its own replacement for a retiring minister. One member of the Federal Council serves a single-year term as president, so that the parties rotate. Compromise is integral to political governance. The cantons are self-governing and guard their independence. Strikes are rare.

Germany has a strong federal constitution and forms national governments by coalitions of the parties: many significant strands of opinion are represented. Only France has a centralised winner-takes-all government like Britain. At least the French know how to riot.

Taxation policy is also a major failure. The last four decades have been marked by constant demands for lower taxes. This has been a creeping complement to austerity, because it has led to stealth cuts, which were initially not noticed. Essential services have been hollowed out. Women are often reduced to taking poor-quality local jobs because of the lack of decent bus services. Too many people drive cars for the same reason. I suspect that British governments economise by dumping higher costs on the individual citizen, without considering the total effect on society, but this is hard to prove.

Sooner or later, Britons will have to decide whether they prefer high-quality public services at higher tax levels, or wish to rely on private provision with many people falling through inadequate safety nets. The second option currently seems to be in the ascendant. Even worse, taxes on the middle classes have been raised while the oligarchs continue to escape contributing their share. It is worth remembering that post-war prosperity was built on an 83% top rate of tax on earned incomes and a 98% top rate on investment incomes. Britain's problem now is that taxes are rising to compensate for a flatlining economy.

THE CUMULATIVE EFFECT OF POLICY FAILURES

It is impossible to establish how much of the decline in living standards has been caused by each separate policy failure, or by financial engineering. Collectively the answer is: they all played a part.

Seven major British policy failures, culminating in a "let's wreck our trade (particularly in services) for decades, hoping to get a trivial benefit later" strategy of economic destruction. Some public services have been affected by more than one of these policy failures. For example, the NHS is struggling because it has been damaged by a combination of the PFI, austerity, and Brexit. Social care was damaged by austerity and Brexit, which fed back into the NHS via bed blocking.

We need to look at how badly Britain's system of political governance has performed. The PFI provides a case study, and Appendix A republishes material that I wrote in 2002 when the official craze for PFI was at its height. But first, let's put this cumulative failure into context by seeing how much living standards have *really* fallen.

MEASURES OF LIVING STANDARDS

Politicians addicted to schoolboy point-scoring always look for the most favourable way to express any statistic, then push that in the media. I choose to measure living standards per person and adjust them by the Retail Price Index (RPI), which better reflects total personal costs than the government's preferred Consumer Price Index. This gives inflation-adjusted comparisons which reflect real living standards.

The following data has been taken from the Office for National Statistics as follows:

GDP   Chained volume method for calendar year
RPI   End December figure each year
Population   Mid-year estimate (only the decennial census gives a more reliable count)

Year	2007	2012	2017	2022
GDP for year £ bn	1,553	1,505	2,182	2,506
Population	61.2m	63.7m	66.0m	67.5m
RPI	203.2	231.5	278.1	360.4

From this we can calculate GDP per person:

At that year's prices	£25,380	£23,630	£33,061	£37,126
At 2007 prices	£25,380	£20,740	£24,157	£20,932

Table 1 - Falling living standards in the UK

Real economic output per person in the UK fell by 17.5% in 15 years. This is the true measure of Britain's failed system of political governance. It would not be a surprise to learn that living standards have since fallen further. This figure includes the aggregate effect of rent-extraction by water company owners through their financial engineering, the extra costs of the PFI compared to exchequer finance, and the hidden costs of austerity such as the NHS, asylum, and court backlogs. It also includes loss of trade and inflation arising from leaving the single market and customs union, the extra interest costs caused by encouraging borrowing through quantitative easing (QE), the loss to the taxpayer from the same scheme (explained later), and of course the Covid-19 pandemic.

How can this be reconciled with statistics that show rising economic output (GDP)? These published statistics are unadjusted for either inflation or population changes. However, such adjustments are only part of the problem. Rewards have flowed to 1% of the population while everyone else has become poorer[7].

PRIVATISATION

This is topical and merits more exploration.

The UK retail energy market

The Office of Gas and Electricity Markets (OFGEM) sets a cap on prices. The cap mechanism was originally designed to protect those consumers who had fixed-price deals coming to an end from price gouging by energy distributors. Many households now pay the capped price, with extra charges for the poorest who use prepayment meters and for those on tariffs that include standing charges. There are extensive spreadsheets on the OFGEM website which I could not decipher. Four issues have emerged, the first two courtesy of Professor Richard Murphy of Sheffield University, the third from a statement by Christine Farnish, who resigned as an external director of OFGEM on the basis that OFGEM was unfairly favouring distributors. The fourth issue was revealed in a news report in *The Independent*. It is possible that some of these points have been subsequently corrected:

1. OFGEM used the international market price for gas as an assumed cost for all UK gas purchases by energy distributors. This does not seem to allow for the lower cost of North Sea gas. Marginal electricity generation is from gas, so it is conceivable that OFGEM may have inflated electricity prices, causing excessive profits for generators and distributors[32].

2. OFGEM's model for price calculation did not apparently vary margins with absolute price levels. Wholesale gas supplies generally account for just under half of distributors' costs. Double those costs, and it seems that suppliers' profits were allowed to rise by a similar percentage (instead of being fixed in cash terms)[33].

3. Because of the steep rise in prices, OFGEM allowed distributors to anticipate further price rises before they happened, to prevent

additional bankruptcies, even though bankruptcy may conceivably be in the public interest[34].

4. The energy supplier, Bulb, failed with debts of £326m. The administrators were debarred by UK law from hedging supply prices and, as a result, the shortfall spiralled to £2.2 bn, which was added to the costs to be recovered by higher prices. Nobody cares[35].

Water

Water is a basic necessity of life. The water companies have drawn attention because of their leaky pipelines, lack of investment in new reservoirs, and sewage pumped into rivers and onto beaches[36].

The nine regional water companies in England and the one in Wales were privatised in 1989, but Welsh water is now a not-for-profit undertaking. There are some other local companies. In England, small shareholders gradually sold out and private equity took over, with the result that 71% of the shares in the nine regional English companies were held outside the UK[37].

Promises made at privatisation included more investment and lower prices for consumers. The opposite happened. Political challenge focuses mainly on the dividends taken out. The analysis that follows is based on specific companies and does not imply relevance to all.

Water company accounts are exceedingly detailed, because of both accounting and the Water Services Regulation Authority (OFWAT) requirements. As a result, it is difficult to work out what is really going on.

Water companies engage in managing financial risks through derivatives. These financial instruments can be used to manage risk, transfer value between entities, or simply for gambling. Thames Water has run a net liability on its derivative positions for some years:

Year	Liabilities £	Assets £
2018	406m	63m
2019	1.2bn	8m
2020	1.0bn	nil
2021	1.5bn	151m
2022	2.2bn	170m
2023	2.0bn	449m

Table 2 - Derivative liabilities and assets at Thames Water

For 2023, the net liability positions indicate that Thames Water owed over £1.5 bn to third parties for its hedging strategies. The notes to the accounts reveal that, in the year to 31 March 2023, Thames Water paid £412.6 m and earned £48.1 m on derivative settlements, a net loss of £364.5 m. The previous year it made a profit of £20.6 m. What is the benefit for the people who matter, their captive customers for water supplies? In 2023, Thames Water shareholders received £45.2 m internal dividends on £1.8 bn equity. About eight times the dividend paid to the group holding company was spent on derivatives. Who profited from this? Accounting standards do not appear to require an explanation.

Thames Water has a high proportion of index-linked debt. The risk that higher inflation would damage this cost structure was overlooked, but it became apparent in summer 2023. It seems that derivatives did not hedge against the actual rise in inflation.

In 2017, The *Financial Times* reported that Macquarie (the then owner of Thames Water), an Australian infrastructure investor, had transferred £2 bn of debt onto the books of Thames Water and had earned 15.5% to 19% annually for eleven years[38]. When I examined the accounts for Thames Water (no longer owned by Macquarie) to 31 March 2022, I found £14.1 bn debt at an interest cost of £312 m. This is an effective rate of 2.2%, supporting the claim that water utilities are a super-safe investment that can borrow very cheaply.

This suggests that the financial structure of Thames Water up to when Macquarie sold out in 2017, was based around large interest payments on debt, which went to the owners by a circuitous route. Those payments would have been deductible for tax, or as the private equity industry calls it: "tax efficient". In effect, the UK taxpayer was subsidising a foreign owner. Excessive returns to the offshore owners, tax concessions, higher consumer prices, and lack of the investment promised at privatisation were all draining the English economy. At least the current financial structure clearly does not incur such artificially high interest costs.

I tried comparing Thames Water to two other large water companies, Severn Trent and Yorkshire. Both these had much smaller derivative liabilities, and their accounts showed that the cause was hedging against energy price changes, interest rates, and currency fluctuations. As an individual observer, it seems to me that hedging energy costs is reasonable. Hedging interest rate risk is also reasonable if it relates to UK loans and bank overdrafts, although I would question its use if it related to loans from a parent company. But currency risk? Why borrow in currencies other than sterling? Or were these loans in private-equity style from the owners, in the owners' currencies? There is no information in the accounts. If true – one hopes not – then the public would be protecting foreign owners from any risk of currency losses via derivative costs, while also paying for sterling depreciation and needing to repay more in sterling when sterling declines. Sterling depreciation brings windfall gains in foreign assets but serious costs in repaying foreign debts. This raises two issues:

1. Unfortunately, accounting standards do not appear to require monopoly businesses to state who benefits from derivative contracts that mature at a profit: the owners or the customers. Nor do we know who profits on the other side of the contract when derivatives mature at a loss.

2. Given that some water companies have possibly been borrowing in foreign currencies, here may be another hidden Brexit cost following the fall in sterling. *Not* a benefit.

This has similarities with the general observation that acquired companies pay their new private equity owner for the 'privilege' of being bought and owned[39].

Privatisation of water was sold to the public as a recipe for more investment, but in the thirty-three years since, no new reservoir has been built in England, and pipeline leaks have reached 20% of all water used. Now the sewage scandal has drawn attention to the inadequacies of water privatisation. A banker who worked on the original privatisations has argued that the key problem was failure to think long term on the part of government and regulator[40].

It is worth mentioning here that the various financial engineering techniques for extracting money from the taxpayer and the public are described in technical detail by Professor Brett Christophers of Uppsala University as "asset manager society"[41]. In my view, neither large political party can achieve significant economic improvement while private equity is allowed to extract money from British society [42].

Rail

Rail is largely a natural monopoly, excepting where two operating companies compete on the same tracks or by different routes between two places. Rail fares in Britain are among the highest in Europe. A standard peak-hour single second-class ticket between Bristol Temple Meads and Paddington costs £126.40 one way for a journey of 167 km (and, unlike in Italy, there is no guarantee of a seat). A similar journey in Switzerland (usually one of the most expensive places to live), say Basel to St. Gallen (164 km), costs £55 at current exchange rates. Regular travellers (about one-third of the population) pay half this using a half-fare annual travel card costing around £150.

In 2017, the TSSA rail union ran a campaign to draw attention to why British train travel is so expensive, unless you tie yourself to a particular off-peak timing weeks ahead. The reason is simple. Many of the operating companies are owned by German railways, Dutch railways, Spanish railways, French railways, Italian railways, and Australian investors. Only those run by First Group are largely British owned. Other countries' railway systems were alleged by TSSA to be overcharging in the UK in order to subsidise their own operations[43]. One of those European operators is now in the process of selling out to private equity.

In the cases of both water and rail, regulators were supposed to ensure value for the British taxpayer. The two stories are very different, but both carry undertones of legislative shortcomings (i.e. introducing doubts about design of the regulations)[44, 45]. The scope of regulators varies. Some (e.g. the Financial Conduct Authority) cover the whole UK. OFGEM has no power in Northern Ireland; OFWAT is restricted to England and Wales. The draft constitution in Chapter 8 leaves the option of pragmatic arrangements open. However, it does impose overdue restrictions on financial engineering.

Energy, water and rail raise some questions as to whether the British model of privatisation has succeeded. Collectively, the effect of draining money out of the British economy via financial engineering is, in my view, a contributing factor in the long-term depression of incomes and rise in poverty.

As we look back on both privatisation and the PFI, we can see why school and hospital buildings are now suffering from neglect. The extra costs of PFI are draining budgets that have also been squeezed by austerity and Brexit. These costs are a factor in the waves of strikes that have affected the health and education services[46]. Everyone pays for thirty years ... or longer.

3 THE CASE FOR CONSTITUTIONAL CHANGE

WHAT MAKES A SOCIETY SUCCESSFUL?

In their book, *When Nothing Works*, five academics from Manchester describe three pillars of society: disposable (or residual) income, essential services, and social infrastructure. All three pillars have been wrecked by deliberate policy choices[47]. The authors show how the three pillars interact. They argue that UK policies are stuck in a quagmire, with too much regulatory weight given to market-oriented economists. The academics show how the share of national output going to employment has fallen by nearly 10% between 1976 and 2019: it is another factor to add to the seven major policy failures, contributing to Britain's poverty problem. The central government keeps control by setting objectives and requiring performance statistics.

This is an example of the many problems with British political governance. Politicians sell aspiration and talk about sharing the proceeds of growth, but deliver declining living standards. To understand what is wrong and how it could be fixed, we need to explore alternative systems of governance. It is no longer good enough to say, "This is how we have always done it."

THE DEAD-END OF POLITICAL EVOLUTION

The detailed evidence shows that privatisation has only been a partial success and has brought a new set of troubles. The PFI looks retrospectively to have been even more financially damaging than I thought it would be in 2002 (Appendix A).

We need to understand why the checks and balances of democracy have failed. Before 1911, the two houses of parliament had substantially equal powers. The upper house was derived from the nobility who counselled kings half a millennium ago. The lower house drew its membership from the people, elected on the basis of who could curry most favour in a constituency. Only men could vote. The world was simpler: no air travel, telephone, radio, TV, or internet.

Lloyd George changed the substantially equal powers, to restrict the power of the Lords so that the lower house could prevail after an interval of a year or so. There was a minor amendment post-war. Then, gradually, local government was changed, and local authorities merged to produce economies of scale. The mirror image of larger local authorities is, of course, remoteness and loss of local interest.

The advent of television and the decline of local newspapers led to centralised government talking to the people through centralised media. The people had few ways to talk back. Consultations became empty charades, leading to the farce of a consultation on restoring imperial measures omitting the option to say "No". Parliamentary petitions are now discarded with inane excuses. For example, a petition to 'Negotiate Re-entry to the Single Market' was rejected with this statement:

"Leaving the EU was the democratic wish of the British public. The Government is now focussed on implementing the Trade and Cooperation Agreement, ensuring it delivers for our citizens and businesses"[48].

The Westminster model of democracy is nothing more than two parties at war, taking turns to impose their world view. No parliament can bind its successors, so legislation is made and unmade. A good example is the endless switches of taxation policy on businesses between full deduction of capital investment (100% first-year allowances, now called 'full expensing') and reduced allowances, which produce an artificial tax charge discouraging new investment. In Britain's unstable governance where taxes can be changed at whim, the claim that this relief will be permanent is sham. It will be cancelled when a future government needs a quick boost to revenue.

Let's digress for a moment and look at the constant changes in policy. Instability is damaging, because nobody can rely on knowing what the rules are. Short-termism always wins over sensibly building the future. It is endemic in Britain. Governments run after fashions (e.g. privatisation, the PFI, austerity) without considering their long-term effects. Cost-cutting is always preferred to quality, so infrastructure is inadequate and maintenance demands rise.

Consider immigration as an example of extreme political instability. The country is desperately short of many workers, not just in healthcare, so visa issuance rose steeply (although the figures are slightly overstated because they are *net* immigration and Britons can no longer move easily to the 31 free-movement countries, which biases the statistics upwards by roughly 50,000 per annum – an unrecognised own goal). A panic about high figures followed, so the government increased pay requirements and announced restrictions to discourage families: a change of policy from recognising the need for immigration, to restricting it. Then it realised this would be counter-productive and eased the proposed family rules. Next, it reverted to the original rules but said they would apply a year later. The exception allowing lower pay for health and social care workers has been retained. Perhaps a new government will adopt a sensible, pragmatic policy and stick to it.

Returning to political evolution, the checks and balances of democracy continued to erode as centralisation spread. Cabinet government was supposed to resolve policy conflicts. Tony Blair introduced sofa government, in presidential style. Mass media then reduced contests between the parties to personalities. Compromise is not only unwanted but driven out by the system. Nuanced points of view are difficult to accommodate in the first-past-the-post electoral system. Only on the rare occasions that hung parliaments arise can any compromise be entertained. A hung parliament may also give rise to extremist capture, as happened to Theresa May's government. The ultimate example is a damaging hard Brexit that few thought they were voting for, or accept now.

Governments have a life-cycle of five stages:

1. The opposition unites as a government in waiting, but says little about proposed policies to avoid schoolboy-level attacks from the other side.
2. Power changes hands, and a new elite acquires the ability to rule like mediaeval kings.
3. The new government tries to fix some things and promote its own ideas.
4. In its middle age, it makes compromises with other points of view.
5. It decays, descends to internal warfare, loses sight of the public interest as minorities dictate policy, and opens the way to the other lot grabbing power.

Once a government loses its cohesion, then any minority of its backbenchers amounting to half its majority can cause mayhem: witness the May and Truss governments and the travails of the Sunak government. Minorities can also capture hopeless oppositions, as we have seen in recent years. The best defence against minority capture is a formalised system of proportional representation (PR), which Britain uses in Scotland, Wales and Northern Ireland but not for the UK parliament. The UK government is often formed from a minority of voters, because first past the post usually creates a winner-takes-all parliament. This is unsatisfactory.

The road to British serfdom

This slow deterioration in the checks and balances that democracy needs has taken over a century. When a general election comes round, each party publishes its manifesto. If one party wins a majority in the House of Commons, it forms a government, and vague policies in its manifesto become inviolable. The people are deemed to have approved them all. This is ridiculous. The people are forced to accept the bundle even if they only want one or two of the expressed policies. The manifesto statements may themselves be unclear and capable of differing interpretations.

The Salisbury convention stops the House of Lords blocking policies that are laid out in the winning party's manifesto. Those policies are usually expressed in vague general terms, using words such as 'review', 'modernise', or 'balance'. The real intent behind them is rarely disclosed. The democratic deterioration has now gathered pace with the adoption of policies ostensibly to deter Channel crossings that were not mentioned in any manifesto. The opposition has said that it will repeal that legislation, which it was constitutionally entitled to oppose as the Salisbury convention did not apply. They abstained on second reading. The House of Lords is ineffective even when it could act.

There have been demands for politicisation of the civil service. Senior officials are fired for speaking truth to power, or instructed to follow orders in contentious cases. Overall, government treats Britons as serfs.

I have recently discovered a good example of British serfdom. When the Bank of England adopted QE, I was concerned that, in order to succeed, the operation had to persuade Britons to take on more debt, which would ultimately prove damaging to household and business finances. Since the Bank was also apparently buying gilts for more than their redemption value, I had a secondary concern: that there could be losses to the public purse. It has come to light that the expected losses on the entire UK QE programme are some £150 bn. These losses are included in public debt forecasts and will be met by the Treasury. To put it in simple terms: because some households were encouraged to take on more debt, the public may pay an extra £150 bn in taxes, spending cuts or borrowing. This is serfdom. Not democracy[49]. In my view, QE has caused more problems than it has solved.

Britain has autocratic governments led by elected dictators. Soft power has been used to make institutions conform to government wishes. Suitable people do not come forward for public appointments because they may be victims of character assassination in the media. And so the standard of political discourse spirals down to entrenched positions, emotional appeals, and personal attacks. Nor does government by publicity stunt amount to sensible political discourse. To talk of leaving the European Convention on Human Rights to deport 200 asylum seekers annually to Rwanda is extreme nonsense. Consult Appendix B to find out what rights you could then have taken from you, to add to restrictions on demonstrations and gerrymandered voting.

Politicians have to appeal for votes with empty slogans, avoiding offending their supposed core voters. Thus, they avoid issues that concern the public and promote unnecessary divisions between people.

Few understand Britain's unwritten constitution. The Privy Council is the ultra-Establishment body. It is used by government as a way of imposing its will without consulting the people: witness the prorogation of parliament in 2019. It can bypass parliament to make legislation. The Privy Council is the beating heart of autocratic Britain. Abolish it.

Of course, the Privy Council has some functions that would still be needed. The Accession Council is defined in my draft constitution. The Judicial Committee is in reality a unit of the Supreme Court; change its name to something like 'Overseas Section of the Supreme Court'. Grants of royal charters should be transferred to the UK parliament and thereby brought under democratic control. However, many bodies listed as having charters that have not been surrendered do not appear to exist: for example, Bucks and Oxon Union Bank is on the list, but was taken over by Lloyds Bank in 1902. A purge of inactive chartered bodies is long overdue.

The House of Lords is a strange mixture of independent technocratic appointments (which generally bring quality to its work), political appointments (sometimes against the advice of the appointments commission), and inherited membership (derived from the nobility). According to Ian Dunt in his book *How Westminster Works and Why it Doesn't*, it allows government to quietly change legislation without anyone noticing[50]. It spends much time trying to improve legislation, only for the government to whip its MPs to overturn Lords' amendments, making it powerless. Since Royal assent is also a charade, there are no effective checks on poor governance or bad legislation until damage has been done.

The mess that Britain is now in cannot be fixed by half-measures of Lords' reform, fiddling with bits of the constitution, unless the entire centralised State is replaced. Government needs to get closer to the people; the people need ways to talk back. PR would help sometimes, should it encourage compromise, but also runs the risk of allowing more extremist capture of major parties. The major parties have to fragment for PR to represent all views.

Very good examples of the mess can be found in the weekly Prime Minister's Questions. Backbenchers raise serious cases of miscarriages of common sense, such as the teenage Georgian boy from Glasgow who was threatened with deportation when orphaned (he has since been allowed to stay in the only place he calls home)[51]. Asylum seekers who are qualified doctors and approved to work by the British regulator have been prevented from working and kept in Home Office accommodation at public expense because of the complete lack of joined-up operational thinking in government[52]. Then there's the case of the Afghan pilot who was threatened with deportation to Rwanda for the sin of being neglected by Britain and therefore taking an irregular route to safety, following empty British promises[53]. It now appears that the original grand aims of the Afghan Relocation and Assistance policy have since been more narrowly defined; politicians took the initial credit then wrote restrictive rules (although there has been a small relaxation for those stuck in temporary accommodation in Pakistan). Did they hope that the public would forget?

The vexed question of asylum is a good example of government failure. The backlog was allowed to grow through neglect (including austerity: downgrading the level of case workers by one grade to save pennies, with a consequential reduction in cases resolved per caseworker). Now the government is believed to be considering throwing a number of asylum seekers upon the strained resources of local authorities, to meet an arbitrary political target and shift the cost elsewhere in the State. A similar process of state buck-passing may occur if a hospital speciality cancels appointments on the grounds that another speciality would be more appropriate; the unlucky person could be sent to the back of the waiting list.

Ideology has no place in providing essential services that are necessary for life. In his introduction to his book[50], Ian Dunt exposes the sorry mess of privatisation of the probation service caused by the combination of ideology and short-termism. The service had to be renationalised after it had been severely damaged. It is just one of many examples of the failure of the present system of political governance.

The rise of political advisers promoting their ideologies and simplistic messages in lieu of impartial advice by civil servants has aided erosion of checks and balances. The result is a travesty of democracy. Only public opinion and the threat of a lost election stand between Britain and dictatorship. This growth of political advisers has coincided with declining standards of discourse, growing unhappiness in the civil service, and promotion of ideological policies. One sometimes wonders whether the high level of policy failures may be connected with the growing number of unaccountable and untrained advisers kept at public expense. Ministers should stand on their own two feet; when they need advice, the civil service should provide it. The number of special advisers should be severely limited.

These incidents and methods damage the British economy, deepen the loss of trust in its governance, stain Britain's international reputation, and continue the slide to autocracy.

OTHER FAILURES

In his book *Follow the Money*[54], the economist Paul Johnson recounts many other British policy failures in the last few decades, but relatively few successes. Common causes for policy failure arise from short-term cost cuts without considering the consequences, or politicians being carried away with the factional interests of their parties. Johnson paints a contrast between universities showered with funding via student loans and further education colleges scraping by on pittances. Britain will never compete with other countries unless it sorts out its continuing training in technical skills.

Then there is the cancellation of the second leg of HS2, which is turning into an expensive railway from nowhere in west London to somewhere in east Birmingham[55]. The losses caused by QE may be contributing to the inability to complete infrastructure, but HS2 would have sucked money out of local transport networks just as effectively as the PFI sucked money out of unlucky schools and hospitals.

One other consequence of the multitude of policy failures is Britain's extreme inequality. Income and wealth inequality causes higher crime levels and other social failures[56]. The meticulous evidence from social scientists was first published in 2009, yet governments since then have persisted in ignoring the evidence. Clearly the need for evidence should be imposed upon most legislation. Instead of a rising prison population, held in ancient inadequate prisons, which are reputed to be universities of crime, the crime problem should be tackled by reducing inequality, its root cause. Traditional party politics have been to soak the rich in support of the poor. But there is another way. The ratio of the highest income to the lowest in any organisation could be restricted, and the restriction progressively tightened. This would gradually bear down on the serious social problems Britain faces.

CLOSING RANKS AGAINST THE TRUTH

A completely different class of government failure arises from the habit of closing ranks against the truth, to protect the organisation. All monopolistic organisations, not just governments, are prone to this. In his book *The Power in the People*[57], the lawyer Michael Mansfield KC exposes a number of cases of silence to avoid the truth. The book covers long-forgotten failures of the criminal justice system, which chime with recent cases such as a conviction for rape overturned after twenty years' imprisonment; among several errors, that particular innocent party had been refused early release because he would not admit his guilt.

Mansfield identifies three common features linking Bloody Sunday, the Marchioness sinking on the River Thames, Hillsborough and Grenfell:

1. "It's not about the nature of the incident, but rather the nature of the governance and the culture it cultivates.
2. It's not governance that recognises the malfeasance and forces change, but the persistence of the people.
3. The malfeasance identified does not arise out of the blue, like some weird aberration that has taken everyone by surprise." *(Reproduced with permission of the Licensor through PLSclear)*

Mansfield quotes examples of how the people have successfully held the powerful to account, and shows that the people can conduct inquiries and discover the truth. His findings are consistent with my proposals, which we will come to in Chapter 5.

A different example of closing ranks against the truth occurs with Brexit. Nobody wants to talk about it. Even achieving a compromise solution would therefore need a campaign possibly lasting decades. The benefits of Brexit are constantly overhyped, leading to further distrust of all politicians. Here are some examples:

1. Britain had freeports when it was in the EU but abolished them in 2012 because they only shifted business around.
2. New free-trade agreements such as with Australia (that were not in place with the EU) give trivial benefits and, in the particular case of Australia, may damage British farming.
3. The new Swiss financial services agreement largely reproduces EU (specifically European Economic Area) benefits, as Switzerland is negotiating for mutual recognition by the EU.

THE DEMOCRATIC DEFICIT

In Britain, the SNP, and to a lesser extent Plaid Cymru, have pushed their own agendas of devolution and independence. The 2014 "No" vote to Scottish independence was influenced by the argument that Scotland would be out of the EU for a decade. The alternative to repeated independence demands is a federal country on the American, Australian, Canadian, German or Swiss models. Scotland could go its own way on taxation, public spending, employment, and social progress, while remaining in a defence, currency, trade and foreign affairs union with the rest of the UK. I will show later that even trade could be *partially* the responsibility of the nations.

Dr Hannah White worked in parliament for a decade and has set out all the many faults of the House of Commons in her book *Held in Contempt: What's Wrong with the House of Commons*. Many of them relate to government control over the business of the House and, when you read the story, amount to a denial of democracy. The Commons cannot debate secondary legislation; the government whips control everything[58]. White describes the failings of politicians, showing how they have led to a broader lack of trust. Yet her ideas, as with many other books analysing Britain's politics, are for relatively small changes within the present system. The latest farce in 2023 was the King's speech: fifty sentences debated for five days, but debates about major legislation are always limited to a few hours. Wrong priorities.

Professor Linda Colley thinks Britain needs reform of parliament, Whitehall (i.e. the civil service), a modern electoral system better reflecting diversity of opinion, stricter controls on corruption and lobbying, and reduced power for activists to choose a prime minister[59]. There is a better way to tackle this extensive democratic deficit: eliminate the entire concept of two parties fighting for absolute unrestricted power.

FEDERAL SYSTEMS OF GOVERNANCE

American federalism has complex roots, since it arose from both independence and the various settler colonies, of which thirteen were British. Other colonies were French and Spanish. Resistance to British sovereignty culminated in the Boston Tea Party of 1773 and the war of independence that followed from 1775 to 1783. The newly formed 'Congress' declared independence in July 1776. These events led to the American constitution, adopted in 1787. Ten amendments, known collectively as the Bill of Rights, were made in 1791. According to Professor Heather Cox Richardson, a contemporary scholar of American history, current fights over the budget and rights of states go back more than a century[60].

Swiss federalism has even more complex roots. Three cantons declared independence from the Habsburg empire in 1291. From then until 1848, a fluctuating number of cantons (each being a sovereign state) were linked by shifting military alliances. In 1847, there was a short civil war, lasting just four weeks, between Catholic and Protestant cantons. The war fizzled out with a general desire to reconcile differences, resulting in a federal government with limited powers set out in a written constitution. The cantons remain sovereign states and, to this day, have power to enter into some international treaties, excluding trade. The constitution has been modified many times since, but the mantra of Switzerland is "Every canton is different".

Canadian and Australian federations were born out of independence from the UK, and both countries have written constitutions originally made by Acts of the UK parliament. If parliament can legislate for federalism and written constitutions in former colonies, then it can certainly do so within the UK.

The case for British federalism is cursorily dismissed as being impossible on two grounds:

1. Five-sixths of the population is in England, making England dominant.
2. It is unnecessary and even counterproductive because a unitary state can transfer resources from stronger to weaker parts.

These are bogus excuses. For the first point, look at the relative populations of California and Wyoming in America: 39.2 million to 579,000. Or consider the population of Zurich compared with Appenzell Innerrhoden: 1.52 million to 16,100[61]. These are more extreme population ratios than England to any of the other three UK nations. The size of England is a questionable argument as it implies that England should have the right to use its numbers to impose its will on the other nations. I will cover the second bogus argument later.

Table 3 (opposite) shows part of Britain's problem. We can see from this that Britain is highly centralised compared to the federal countries. Every British government department and agency has its own structure, local government spends central money according to central diktat, and face-to-face contact with anybody having decision-making authority requires lengthy journeys. No wonder citizens are alienated.

There are three other factors in citizen alienation: freedom of speech, the right to avoid self-incrimination, and constitutional law that is accessible and comprehensible (Table 4, opposite).

As explained in Appendix B, freedom of speech is somewhat limited in Britain. Self-incrimination now occurs by law: the English common law right to silence has been replaced by the presumption that silence means guilt in these cases:

- for alleged terrorism
- for alleged fraud
- generally in Northern Ireland and
- generally by the Criminal Justice and Public Order Act 1994.

	America	Australia	Canada	Switzerland	Britain
Tax-raising	Divided	Part central	Divided	Divided	Central
Expenditure	Divided	Divided	Divided	Divided	Central (UK has a limited exception for Scotland)
Internal Competition	Some	Some	Some	Yes	No
Language by state	No	No	Yes	Yes	No
States make own law	Yes	Yes	Yes	Yes	Limited, can be overruled
Centre can overrule	No	Superior	No	No	Yes

Table 3 - Comparisons of federal and devolved states

	America	Australia	Canada	Switzerland	Britain
Freedom of speech	Yes	Case law	Yes	Yes	Limited
Avoid self-incrimination	Yes	Case law	Yes	Yes	Exceptions
Written constitution	Yes	Mixed	Mixed	Yes	Incomprehensible

Table 4 - Further comparisons of federal and devolved states

It is almost impossible for any citizen to understand the British constitution. It consists of a mixture of legislation, sometimes going back for centuries, together with amendments to that legislation. Add to the mix assorted conventions — how many citizens even know what the Salisbury convention is about? — Crown privileges and prerogatives (very different), the Privy Council, and many official committees that have a constitutional effect. I doubt that many of the people who believe in parliamentary sovereignty even realise that it excludes many international matters, which are largely Crown prerogative powers and therefore exercised by the executive government in the name of the Crown. *Not* the people.

Federal countries also seem to do better in involving the citizen. The Swiss have many referenda: all major legislation, including constitutional change and some international treaties, requires approval by the people. Voluntary approval (when either the federal or a cantonal government calls a referendum without being obliged to do so) and popular initiatives (when sufficient voters demand a referendum) are also part of Swiss democracy. The people make government policy. In 2019, the Swiss courts annulled a taxation referendum held in 2016 because the federal government had made a mistake in its data[62].

American states have their propositions: Australia uses referenda. Direct democracy is a key component of those three federations. In Britain, however, the people's opinion is largely unwanted. There is no protection against mistakes or lies, nor is there even a requirement for a majority of the nations to agree. Note that America imported the first-past-the-post electoral system and the model of two tribes competing for power from Britain. The American model has its own limitations.

A federal structure does not need direct democracy: Canada is the example. However, for direct democracy to flourish, a federal structure is preferable. Power must be dispersed rather than concentrated, reducing the influence of centralised media and lobbyists. One person, one vote. *Not* one pound, one vote.

We also need to consider the vexed issue of taxation and public expenditure. All four federal countries allow the individual states to raise taxes and determine their own expenditure, although Australian states receive some central subsidies. In Switzerland, the financially strong cantons subsidise the weaker ones through an inter-cantonal support fund. The objection that a central British State is needed so that England can support the weaker parts does not stack up. People should vote for the principle; the detail should be determined in relation to measured differences reviewed regularly, instead of depending on the political calculations of over forty years ago (which is the present position with the Barnett formula, whereby England provides financial support to Scotland). This raises another point, relevant to the size-of-England argument. England itself encompasses strong and weak regions. Any financial support mechanism should therefore be regional as well as between the nations. Levelling up solved.

In learning from other federations, there is one final point. History matters. All were born out of some sort of independence movement, or a civil war. Britain is now following a well-trodden path. Disillusion with politicians, disillusion with the Establishment, may lead to some sort of fracture. American independence arose because the King (i.e. the Westminster government) was seen as tyrannical. Nothing new there.

From this we can deduce some simple factors for successful federations:

1. Every federation is a unique solution to conflicts in history, geography, culture and language.

2. Successful federations:

    (a) balance the powers between the centre and the states

    (b) allow ongoing changes

(c) involve the people

(d) allow component states to raise their own taxes and determine their own expenditure

(e) encourage both internal competition and cooperation.

Now let's see how devolution in the UK measures up:

1. Devolution is unequal between the four nations. Change only happens when Scotland threatens to leave or the factions in Northern Ireland oppose one another. The people are only involved rarely, notably when the Tory party is divided. The nations cannot raise their own taxes and decide how to spend those taxes (Scotland has limited variation powers, while Wales needs permission from London first); internal competition is discouraged by a cult of statist uniformity; cooperation is avoided, even unwanted. The differences between the four nations, notably inward-looking England compared to outward-looking Scotland, make the seniority of London irritating. British devolution fails the success tests.

2. There are particular factors that either encourage or support Britain's extreme centralisation. The civil service is addicted to central control, the electoral system produces an elected dictatorship, and UK-wide media strongly influence politics. The last point was demonstrated clearly in two books[63]. English powers for local authorities (e.g. the 'Northern powerhouse') are countermanded by new centralised functions such as academy schools. Note that Scotland is itself highly centralised; the SNP has replaced Westminster control with even tighter Holyrood control.

3. There are three legal issues: Crown immunity, the royal (or Crown) prerogative, and Orders in Council, which together can be used to impose the will of government. They do not belong in any

democracy, let alone a federal structure. It is past time to sweep all these undemocratic powers away. They *prevent* parliament from being sovereign.

4. There is an emergent structure of tribes that cross national borders within the UK. This is the result of multiculturalism: a series of ethnicities, speaking other second languages, scattered throughout the UK. Instead of the language and cultural issues being geographically contained, as in Canada and Switzerland, the UK has language and cultural differences spread around all four nations. The only language/culture groups that exist within the nations are Welsh speakers in Wales, Scots Gaelic speakers in the Highlands and Islands, and Irish Gaelic speakers in Northern Ireland. According to the 2021 census[64], the fifteen most prominent languages of non-English native speakers in England and Wales are:

Polish	611,845	Gujarati	188,856
Romanian	471,954	Italian	161,010
Panjabi	290,745	Tamil	125,363
Urdu	269,849	French	120,259
Portuguese	224,719	Lithuanian	119,656
Spanish	215,062	Chinese	118,271
Arabic	203,998	Turkish	112,978
Bengali	199,495		

Table 5 - Non-native languages in the UK

In this respect the UK differs from the federal countries.

5. There are British groups that fight corruption[65], and Britain does suffer extensive lobbying (but rarely for the silent majority of voters). A federal structure combined with a written constitution will diminish the power of lobbying.

6. Every British referendum requires a Herculean effort to get one-off legislation through parliament. There is no general capability in British law for the people to be heard.

7. Britain has another peculiar problem that inhibits federalism: the Treasury hates hypothecation, that is allocating particular taxes to specific expenditures. In Switzerland, there were two federal referenda about transport:

   (a) One (24 November 2013) was to increase the motorway tax from CHF 40 to CHF 100 per annum, with an exception for tourists crossing Switzerland, and spend the proceeds on new motorways. 60.5% of the people voting said "No". All cantons had a majority against the proposition.

   (b) Then on 9 February 2014 a referendum to raise federal taxes and spend the increase on capital investment in the railways passed with 62% of the votes and all but one canton in favour.

   We can see that hypothecation, letting people relate taxes to expenditure, works. It involves the people.

8. Britain has almost no internal competition between nations and regions, although a tiny amount was emerging pre-pandemic in healthcare, where different statist solutions were on offer in Wales and Scotland, from those in England.

9. England alone has no parliament. Its representation and governance are intertwined with the UK functions of the Westminster parliament and government. England desperately needs to escape its adversarial politics and false dividing lines.

10. The job of prime minister is too demanding and therefore difficult to fill with an outstanding-quality statesperson. Some prime ministers may even have contributed to British decline[66].

11. We can also see that Scottish devolution and English votes for English laws are little more than power struggles between potential dictators. A proper federal UK will need to grasp issues that are being ignored:

   (a) the success factors that are missing or inadequate: balancing the powers, allowing ongoing changes, involving the people, letting member nations raise their own taxes and determine their own spending priorities, encouraging internal competition

   (b) ensuring that the people are properly informed and the people's voice is heard at the right time on all major issues

   (c) dealing with crown immunity, crown prerogative, the Privy Council, and the House of Lords

   (d) guaranteeing freedom of speech, citizens' rights, and ending the official abuse of immigrants, refugees, and the poorest members of society

   (e) addressing the dominant size of England versus the other nations, which would allow expression to movements such as the Northern Independence Party through regional government

   (f) encouraging political and governmental compromises rather than extremism.

The devolved governments have some powers but Whitehall exercises tight control over them, partly through taxation, and *in extremis* via refusing royal assent to legislation. Compromise mechanisms are limited to memoranda of understanding. Those mechanisms were overruled from the centre when powers were transferred from the EU to the UK. The people were not consulted.

BORDERS

At this point, we need to consider what the impact of borders would be should Scotland leave the UK. Given the current travails of the SNP, this may seem irrelevant. Anything but so.

Perhaps not in the immediate general election, but in a future one, any small party may hold the balance of power in a new parliament. Perhaps two could jointly. This would become more likely if a new government elected in 2024 disappoints, by not grasping the issues holding Britain back. All that is needed is for the SNP to be in a position to dictate terms for a referendum on independence; they wish to act constitutionally so that Scotland can rejoin the EU without risking a Spanish veto.

Assuming nothing changes in England, borders would be simple while an independent Scotland was outside the EU. If Scotland diverged on either trade agreements or visa and residence rights, then customs and/or passport checks would become necessary. Air travellers would find similar controls as they do travelling today to Europe; road travellers would have to stop rather like they do at Dover; rail checks could be done on moving trains.

However, change would come should Scotland join the EU. Hadrian's Wall would then become an external EU border. We know from past experience in Europe what border checks would follow. They would particularly affect rail travellers, since trains would need inspecting at border stations. Embarking passengers would wait in a pen, for gates to open once the train has been inspected. Disembarking passengers would be routed through a customs hall. Platform alterations at Preston and Berwick would be needed. The station wait in cross-border trains before Switzerland joined Schengen was twenty to thirty minutes.

Of course, if England (with Wales and Northern Ireland) then chose to become a free-movement country and join the Schengen area, checks would be reduced to customs only and could again be carried out on moving trains. If England joined the customs union but stayed outside the single market, passport and goods checks would still be needed, as at the Turkish border with the EU.

Borders cause bottlenecks.

DIRECT DEMOCRACY

A federal structure is the most important change Britain needs. There is a role for direct democracy, with citizens (and in some cases, permanent residents) able to express their views.

The reality is that Britain's lack of a written constitution suits the two main parties, because they can change the law as much as they like when in power as elected dictators. This is why Britain has a self-serving, elite Establishment and why Britons have so few rights. But the role of parties has to change. They should propose and gather support for popular initiatives, as well as campaign to form governments.

There is plenty of scope for citizens' initiatives in Britain, to challenge the Establishment. Here are three examples:

1. Establish the basis of national and regional financial support
2. Enforce climate protection.
3. Prohibit the bureaucracy from mission creep without legislation.

Bundling policies together for a general election has failed. The parties now seem to be offering hard-right autocracy versus centrist managerialism, with the fringe more concerned with recovering some traditional seats that voted "Leave" than offering policies that may appeal to many voters. Citizens need to be able to set the agenda without tortuous campaigns. Hence there is a role for citizens to demand referenda at the UK level, subject to threshold support and quality requirements. The ultimate example of this is to agree, and amend, a written constitution.

Use of referenda at national, regional and local level is a matter for the sovereign nations. It needs some common rules, but adoption should be discretionary – with three exceptions:

1. A nation that does not adopt referenda for its internal affairs would still participate in UK referenda.

2. Replacing royal assent by the people's assent could sometimes need to go to a vote, at the discretion of the People's Council.

3. Since boundary changes could cross nations, these also ought to be approved by vote.

Broader economic issues

In order to complete our investigation of federalism and direct democracy in the UK, we need to look at the effect of some much broader economic issues that might be seen differently if the people had more say.

I have long criticised the financial policies followed by governments over the past four decades. Credit has been expanded in the false belief that economic growth could thereby be purchased. Instead, personal and business debt has expanded, and now the cost of debt service is throttling western economies and Japan. I have shown in my book *The Financial System Limit*[67] that debt cannot expand to infinity. That book also explains the concept of the central banking economic cycle, driven entirely by central bank policies. Note also the specific argument made by Professor Mark Blyth[21] that the bank bail-outs of 2008 and 2009 have been paid for by squeezing the poorest.

This failure runs deep. Neo-liberalism was espoused forty years ago as a new economic theory, that the rich should be allowed to spend what they like, and such spending would somehow trickle down to everyone else. A more accurate assessment would note that credit expansion, culminating in QE, has artificially boosted asset prices (including making housing unaffordable) and, equally artificially, provided the finance for a boom in household and consumer borrowing. The very poor are now being squeezed even more by austerity and inflation. For those who wish to learn about it, I also list references to several other books[68]. The younger middle classes are burdened by debt service and repayment. Most of the global economy is now slowing down, and the debt burden will soon matter. Neo-liberalism and inequality are failed aspects of the credit expansion binge. As austerity spreads and debt problems proliferate, asset prices based on credit availability will fall.

OVERSEAS TERRITORIES

The UK has a variety of territories remaining from the days of Empire:

1. ten countries, including Gibraltar, listed by the United Nations as non-self-governing territories[69]
2. three uninhabited possessions (British Indian Ocean Territory, British Antarctic Territory, and South Georgia & the South Sandwich Islands)
3. the sovereign bases in Cyprus
4. the Crown dependencies (Jersey, Guernsey including Alderney and Sark, and the Isle of Man).

The total population of the ten in the first group is about 270,000, varying from 40 (Pitcairn) to 78,554 (Cayman Islands). The smaller territories need financial support. Some of the territories, including uninhabited islands, are key military bases for the UK or USA.

All four groups rely on the UK military for defence, and all four groups are represented diplomatically by the UK Foreign Office, although Jersey executes most foreign affairs itself. None of the groups has representation in parliament. The first and last groups have their own governments for other matters, although deeper analysis shows that they are inextricably linked with the UK. The link for the first group is generally the Privy Council, while for the last it is the monarchy itself.

There should be an associated form of membership for the overseas territories, that requires them to adopt the same minimum standards as the rest of the UK, with economic variations according to living standards only. This would put paid to the selective choice of standards that allows tax havens to masquerade as parts of Britain when it suits them and as independent at other times.

The real nature of the British State is revealed by Gibraltar. According to British politicians, Gibraltar is an independent country with its own constitution that has a UK defence guarantee. Spain argues that it is a British colony that properly should be part of Spain. Brexit has pushed Gibraltar towards Spain.

When you read the Gibraltar constitution, what do you find? There are reserve powers held by the Privy Council throughout. The Gibraltar constitution is an Order in Council made by the Privy Council in 2006, not an Act of either the UK or Gibraltar parliaments. The Governor can write any bill and force it into law (Section 34), dissolve parliament in the interests of good government (Section 38), and executive authority vests in the Crown (section 44). The Governor has the final say in ministerial appointments (section 46) and is responsible for external affairs, defence, internal security and the police (section 48). The Governor can veto the appointment of a Commissioner of Police (section 48) and disregard the advice of the Public Service Commission (section 54). Final appeals go to the Privy Council (section 66). Buried in Annex 2 is power for the Crown to make any law and change the constitution[70].

LINKING THE ISSUES

I will conclude this investigation of the case for British federalism by bringing together the failure of neo-liberalism, the damage done by debt creation, and the spread of austerity.

The pressures caused by the two key issues for the future – excessive private sector debt and climate change – are likely to mount. Britain's elected dictatorship will not be able to cope. Immigration and Europe are already bogeymen. Britain's public services are stretched without European workers, notably doctors and nurses. Britain has long failed to train enough high-quality medical professionals. Fixing this through more training places will take at least two decades. Some specialities cannot carry the training overhead without more European workers, but no European worker will pay visa fees and surcharges when she/he has 30 other countries to consider, with no downsides. This is why any politician promising to fix healthcare without rejoining the single market is hiding the truth. The NHS cannot recruit specialities from poor countries lacking them, only from Europe. Or America.

The British system of endless centralised agencies tripping over one another in the conflict between training and cost-cutting was exposed nearly a decade ago. The NHS regulator for England told hospitals only to fill "essential" vacancies as most hospitals were heading for serious financial deficits. The posts that become vacant most frequently are training placements for newly qualified doctors, who have to serve four six-month hospital placements before choosing whether to specialise or become general practitioners. One-fifth of English training places were left unfilled at 1 August 2015 (one of the changeover dates) as hospitals tried to cut staffing levels. Such is the stupid short-termism delivered by British bureaucrats on behalf of a political system that is incapable of looking beyond a five-year parliamentary term and struggles to plan for longer periods than twelve months. I have little confidence in the NHS workforce plan changing this.

Eventually, debts will have to be destroyed somehow. They can be written off deliberately, making creditors share the losses: this is the Cypriot model, in which all those who had more than €100,000 in the bank were relieved of some of their money. One day, many compensation schemes will run out of funds or run out of the ability to pass more bail-out costs onto other financial businesses. One way or another, credits will be cancelled to pay the debts. There is no other way out. Ideas being floated for extended compensation will simply lead to bank nationalisation, with the underlying problem of "Who pays?" left unsolved.

Absent a planned and democratically agreed cancellation of credits, the economy will drift towards chaos. Those starving as a result of austerity will be augmented by those not earning enough to service unaffordable debt. Meanwhile, climate change will wreak biblical havoc on living standards. The emerging problem with the environment is that net zero targets are woefully inadequate. Much faster progress is needed to preserve the planet.

This is the route to strife. America took 18 years from the Boston tea party to the Bill of Rights. Switzerland took 26 years to get its constitution right after the initial settlement in 1848. Under the pressure of a global depression induced by the cost of servicing private sector debt, the present British constitution may cause Britons to turn on one another. Here is the real danger highlighted by the continual Scottish independence campaigns and the rises of Reform on the far right and Momentum on the far left.

4 OUTLINE OF A SOLUTION

How, then, could Britain reinvent its democracy? In the conflict between rationality and emotion, how can more people make rational decisions?

A written constitution on its own, without federalism, would help a little, but not solve the deep problem of England forming 84% of the population. Only a federal structure can balance the different needs and outlook of the four nations.

The people need to examine the basic principles of federalism and hold a referendum on whether to adopt a federal, written constitution including an element of direct democracy. This alone needs leadership, because it will take time for the public to understand the benefits of federalism. There is no place in a federal structure for the present House of Lords. Existing proposals for a replacement body are misleading: they praise the revising function of the Lords while omitting to mention that many changes are rejected by the whipped majority in the Commons.

The key benefits of federalism would be:

1. Decisions would be closer to the people, who could contribute ideas.

2. Nations and regions could follow policies suited to their own best interests.

3. Many existing politicians could move from the UK level to one of the nations.

4. The existing career path for politicians would shorten, and good people would be more likely to come forward.

5. The honours system of patronage could wither.

6. A simple cash transfer mechanism could replace all funding formulae, allowing nations to achieve more equality in personal living standards.

7. More time could be spent scrutinising legislation (the Commons does not do this[50]).

There is one overarching benefit of federalism. The need for a strong person to hold everything together at the centre disappears. Recent times have shown that prime ministers are human, can make mistakes, and can be dominated by factions in their own parties. Why then do we allow one person to have absolute power? Why do we allow a change of person at the top to cause a complete change of policies? *Without democratic consent?* The person at the centre should represent the entire UK on the international stage, rather than being preoccupied with manoeuvres for domestic advantage.

Let's consider some of the above points in more detail:

1. Instead of having a few hundred full-time members of parliament to scrutinise central government, and powerless local authorities that the English political parties use as a training ground, many more people could participate in democratic government, some on a part-time basis. Where regions are adopted, regional governments would not need full-time membership. The next chapter will

introduce a replacement for autocratic bodies, including provision for part-time participation by the people. This would enable voters generally to play a greater part in democracy. Young people would be able to influence their own future rather than being hostages to older voters with a different outlook.

2. Providing complete local control over all economic matters (to regions in England, and to the other nations) would allow joined-up thinking about transport, health, education, housing, planning, labour visas, and economic incentives. Minimum standards should generally be set at the UK level and then the nations/regions be freed to pursue their own best interests. Endless advisory committees and cross-departmental civil service committees in London can give way to proper local needs. If the West of England wants to recruit multilingual Europeans to work in its tourist industry, it should be able to do so without Whitehall permission. If the farmers of the South East want fruit pickers, why should Whitehall say "No"? If the manufacturing cities in the Midlands and North want to offer incentives such as tax concessions or building permits for businesses, together with housing, a skilled workforce, and more resilient public transport, let them do so.

3. A simple cash transfer mechanism between levels of government based on equality of living standards, so that the lowest level of government has the possibility of allowing everyone to keep themselves, could replace all funding formulae. Why should a council that needs to repair potholes go begging for a share of the pothole fund[71]? Why should councils fight one another across Whitehall desks for a share of taxes raised from their populations[72]? Why should the governing party be able to divert funding to where it offers the best voting prospect[73]? All these are nonsenses; some, democratic outrages.

LEARNING FROM THE GROSS MISTAKE

The Westminster model failed when it collided with the Brexit referendum. Only England and Wales voted "Leave", the latter very narrowly. Scotland, Northern Ireland, and Gibraltar voted "Remain". The numeric majority of England was allowed to impose its will on Scotland, Northern Ireland, and Gibraltar.

This mistake happened because there is no written constitution. The Cameron government whipped its members of parliament to vote down an amendment to the EU Referendum Bill in a debate on 16 June 2015 that would have required all four nations (excluding Gibraltar) to vote "Leave" for the referendum to be valid. David Lidington, the minister sponsoring the Bill, argued that the UK joined the EU as one state and therefore should choose whether to leave as one state on a simple majority. The idea of requiring a majority of three of the five affected nations (including Gibraltar) to vote "Leave" was never considered. Excluding Gibraltar from the defeated amendment itself was interesting: was it because Gibraltar would inevitably vote "Remain", or was it colonialism[74]?

There is a continuing misunderstanding about referenda which has led to questioning whether they should play a part in British democracy. According to the Institute for Government and Bennett Institute for Public Policy[11], referenda are either highly divisive because of their binary nature, or fail to attract sufficient support with low turnout questioning the result. This is inadequate thinking. Referenda could be linked, so that one is contingent on the result of another (which has happened in Switzerland); they could be multiple choice; there could be a threshold minimum turnout or minimum positive vote required to pass (the latter is used in Italy). The gross mistake of the Cameron government was to pitch a definite alternative ("Remain") against an undefined alternative ("Leave"). That is what can happen when you allow any parliament, i.e. any autocracy, to make it up as it goes along.

Britain deserves better. The draft constitution in Chapter 8 provides for referenda at the UK level for common matters, while leaving national and local referenda as an option for the sovereign nations.

A linked referendum on Brexit would have asked first: "Do you want to keep the present relationship with Europe or leave the European institutions and surrender any influence?" The second question, counted only if the first voted "Leave", would have asked: "Do you want to stay in the single market and customs union or change to only having a trade agreement in goods with Europe, largely excluding services?"

A multiple-choice referendum would have been even more effective and refined. It could have been worded as in Figure 1.

Cross one box in the first column. If you would like an alternative to be considered should your choice not gain 50% of the votes cast, also cross a different box in the second column.

I wish to:	My first choice	My second choice
Keep the present relationship with Europe and British influence in Europe	☐	☐
Leave the institutions, but stay in the Single Market and Customs Union	☐	☐
Leave the institutions and Customs Union, but stay in the Single Market only	☐	☐
Leave the institutions, Single Market, and Customs Union with a trade agreement	☐	☐

Figure 1: Example of a multi-choice referendum

We can only speculate as to what the outcome of either linked or multiple-choice referenda might have been. The real lesson is that there has to be a truly independent body to ensure any referendum question is properly addressed as to its possible outcomes.

SOVEREIGNTY

Sovereignty is the Crown in Parliament. According to the same report, the central constitutional principle of the UK is: parliament is sovereign and can therefore make and unmake any laws. Not quite correct. In my view, the central constitutional principle is that the electorate chooses a government based partly on media impressions, partly on slogans, partly on allegiances, and partly on policies. The chosen government is then given absolute power akin to the divine right of Kings to do as it likes, through its control of the House of Commons.

The sovereignty issue can be easily solved, by redefining it as sovereignty of the people of each of the nations comprising the UK. The federal State would therefore be the collective will of the sovereign nations on matters of common interest.

The constitutional effect of the Brexit referendum was that England asserted its right to dictate terms to the other nations of the UK, using a simple majority of all votes. This imposed English colonialism on Scotland and Northern Ireland, and also Wales if repeated in future. Left unchallenged, this will mutate into normal practice. Despite the current travails of Scottish nationalism, there can be no future in English majoritarianism.

I have long thought that Brexit was about Britain (particularly England) stripping itself of its imperial delusions. This will become more obvious when Britain, eventually, tries to repair the damage caused by Brexit and finds that it has little negotiating power beyond the Irish problem. The tedious negotiations over rejoining Horizon Europe may be an early sign of how, deprived of influence, Britain will have to sacrifice its longstanding colonial practices such as cherry-picking parts of an international agreement. Because here was another mistake: nobody knew what Brexit meant[75]. This ignorance, combined with minority capture of the governing party, prevented compromise.

COMPETE, COMPROMISE, COOPERATE, AND CONSULT

Highly centralised government is incapable of handling the complexities of the modern world. We expect superhuman leaders to manage an impossible array of tasks. The electorate makes simplistic choices, nurtured by centralised media and three-word slogans. Thus the 2019 general election was apparently decided between two slogans: "Not Jeremy Corbyn" and "Get Brexit done". The first led to electing a disorganised, even chaotic, government[66]; the second to an ultra-hard Brexit that few desired and was never put to the people. Among the victor's baggage was a manifesto that promised various "reviews" and "modernisations" but never said explicitly that the new government would strip Britons of many rights[18]. Nonetheless, that manifesto was deemed incapable of opposition in the Lords and so European citizens became British subjects - subjects of an autocratic executive in which parliament had, and still has, little influence. So much for sovereignty.

We expect too much from prime ministers and their cabinets. In a conference organised by the Constitution Unit at University College London[76], the former minister Sir David Lidington admitted that senior ministers are pressed with urgent or important decisions and there are always people clamouring for fifteen minutes of their time. Unwittingly, he thereby made the case for federation.

A written constitution for a federal and regional state, with clearly defined responsibilities, would resolve these difficulties. Competition between nations and regions would bring economic growth. Compromise particularly needs to be valued and encouraged, cooperation is essential, and the people should be consulted widely. The entire public sector needs to be a learning organisation for the future – one which does not forget lessons learnt – rather than a protection device for the powerful.

The people need to be able to put issues onto the political agenda without expensive long campaigns. Women's emancipation took a century and included incidents that today we call terrorism. Now many campaigns are trying to get the Establishment to see sense about Brexit. In the two-party system politicians have to avoid offending 'core voters' and also to avoid giving hostages to fortune to be exploited in the media, so they evade recognising public opinion and sidestep questions. Campaigning is necessary but wasted effort when the people have no right to be consulted. Only Northern Ireland has any right to be consulted, enshrined in the Belfast Agreement of 1998, regarding reuniting with the Irish Republic[77]. The other nations have no such rights. English regions have been given political platforms (elected mayors) without commensurate powers.

Devolution is a mess. The very word implies crumbs from the high table. Apart from the special problems of Northern Ireland and the different relationship with the overseas territories, all national components of a federal state should have equal powers.

In the idealised world, nations (and in the case of England, regions) would control all major functions apart from defence, foreign affairs, the currency, trade (possibly with exceptions), and minimum standards. Localising control, especially to English regions, frees people to do what they do best. Economic growth once came from national government attracting major industries, such as car assembly, to Britain. Brexit has destroyed such opportunities, so growth can only come from local initiatives. Hence the need for national sovereignty and English regions.

But the British government exercises control in the style of the Roman military. Every function has a command post in Whitehall, and then units spread around the country, answerable to the centre. It's an obsolete and inefficient model of organisation.

The concept of 'matrix management' has been understood for over half a century. Local units from different functions work together for the common good. They take their functional knowledge and standards from a specialist central department: essentially how best to do something rather than "This is what you are ordered to carry out". This is how federal systems can be made to work effectively. Cooperation, not confrontation. With an element of competition added, to avoid statist centralised solutions. Let's call it cooperative competition.

All the various boards, units, and regional offices of central control need to be merged into the appropriate local government. Standards would remain central. Training units and inspectorates should stay central for efficiency; operational management of everything else should be local. Secure document preparation should again remain central, with authorisation for their issue controlled by the nations or regions (for example, passports by the nations, but work visas by the regions where these exist, otherwise by the nations).

The people need the right to be consulted, the right to choose individual policies, and the duties for politicians to compromise and cooperate. All these have to be provided in a new constitution.

Defining each of the peoples of England, Scotland, Wales, and Northern Ireland as sovereign, would make the UK a union of equals. The common functions, notably defence, would be held on behalf of the sovereign nations. The UK government would have only those functions given to it by the people. Everything else is for the nations to decide. Some functions belong to regions, especially in England, although I suspect that other nations may also find benefits in a regional structure at a later date, once experience has been gained.

Sovereignty means that a progressive forward-looking nation can choose to adopt liberal laws, while a regressive backward-looking nation can choose illiberal laws. There is no need for a one-size-fits-all set of domestic policies.

Asylum should be a matter for the sovereign nations; it is a good example of the benefits of making the nations sovereign. One nation can choose to offer asylum visas (thereby ending the small boats nonsense, itself a consequence of losing the deterrent effect of the

EU Dublin Regulation with Brexit) while another puts up barriers, preferring economic shrinkage as its population ages.

Here are three other reforms that could strengthen sovereignty of the people:

1. Create a body vetting official and political communications so as to eliminate spin and bias. Financial industry communications have to be clear, fair, and not misleading by law. The same principle should apply to government, political campaigns, and the media. For example, a think tank report on climate change included errors that were subsequently corrected; one newspaper published a correction, four others cited the original errors but did not correct them[78]. The requirement for clear, fair, and not misleading communications would put a stop to artificial intelligence (AI) fakery and false use of statistics.

2. Allow electronic voting and multiple-choice voting. In the digital age, the antique procedures of the present electoral system and parliament should be considered anew.

3. Rethink funding of political parties. Annual democratic vouchers could be given to the electorate to donate to a party of their choice. The total income of parties includes all their accounting units, many of which are local unincorporated associations. From the tables of accounts on the electoral commission website[79], I estimate the total as around £150 million annually, perhaps more in general election years: say, £5 per elector annually, a small price to pay for ending the power of donations. Of course, some could refuse to use their vouchers. This proportion, once settled in, could be used to adjust the voucher value.

The *clear, fair, and not misleading* principle puts responsibility for preventing the spread of misinformation on government, politicians, and the media. The mainstream and citizens' media generally publish high-quality journalism. Social media will have to make a serious effort to stop the spread of misinformation. Their proprietors have a responsibility to society.

The overseas territories and Crown dependencies should be represented in the UK parliament, since this will be responsible for their defence, foreign affairs, and standards. The smaller territories by population could share one representative by rotation, and the larger territories have one each. 30,000 population is a good cut-off point: there are several smaller states in the world by population. This would give individual representation to Bermuda, the British Virgin Islands, the Cayman Islands, Gibraltar, Guernsey, Jersey, the Isle of Man, and the Turks and Caicos Islands. Seven less-populated territories would share rotating representation.

THE NUMERICAL DOMINANCE OF ENGLAND

So far as I know, there is no federal state in the world where 84% of the entire population lives in one component nation. This issue needs a unique solution. England needs a greater say than Northern Ireland without using its numbers to dictate its will. There are simple ways to achieve this in a multi-member federation. The American solution is two members of the upper house per state and a lower house based on population. Australia follows a similar principle but with constraints on the relative sizes of the two houses. Switzerland uses the American method, but six out of 26 cantons only have a single upper house representative, and count in pairs for federal referenda.

My proposed solution for the unique problem of English numerical dominance is to allocate representation using segments of the Fibonacci series. This series of numbers is defined by every number being the sum of the two previous numbers, starting with either 0,1 or 1,1 (it does not matter which). Thus the early numbers in the series are:

0, 1, 1, 2, 3, 5, 8, 13, 21, 34, 55, 89, 144, 233, 377, 610...

This series has some unusual properties. The one that matters to us is that the ratio of any number to its predecessor gradually approaches the golden ratio in art, demonstrating aesthetic beauty. Thus 610 divided by 377 is 1.61804; a more precise value for the golden ratio is 1.61803398874989484820. What could be fairer than aesthetic beauty? The practical result is that the largest member nation gets extra representation but can be outvoted in a federation of four or more nations. If there are only three nations, then it can be encouraged to compromise. Adding a small number of representatives for the overseas territories affects this, since the largest member among three nations can then be outvoted.

Thus a representative assembly might consist of eight Northern Irish members, thirteen Welsh members, twenty-one Scottish members, and thirty-four English members, seventy-six in total (plus the overseas territories). This is just an illustration of how the '84% are English' problem could be easily solved[80].

CENTRAL OR LOCAL? WHO PAYS THE PIPER?

Since nations would be sovereign, they can choose what taxes to levy and how to apply them. Nations could allow local governments to raise their own revenue. Each level of government would raise the money it needs, so far as possible. Sovereign nations would make their own laws in everything they have not agreed to share, within the terms of a federal constitution.

Nonetheless, there would be serious differences in living standards, and there needs to be an agreed mechanism to handle those differences. The vexed question of supporting deprived areas has been given new impetus by Brexit. Instead of EU regional funds, promises were made of replacement funds. In an insult to the electorate, those promises were devalued.

British government today has endless different funds and funding formulas, of which the pothole fund[71] is one of the more absurd. Every funding formula needs to be swept away. Instead, there should be an inter-nation equalisation fund and equalisation funds within the nations. These equalisation funds will be two-way, so that financial equalisation is automatic, rather than depending on the munificence of the top level of government. Regional governments could create a third tier for local authorities, using the same principles. Regions freed to promote their own economic development might not need so much financial support in the future. Where there are no regional governments, the national government should provide equalisation between local authorities.

Equalisation funding should seek to bring the average per-capita GDP of weaker parts close to the level of stronger parts. The nations would control transfers between regions and local governments. Equalisation funding only indirectly affect households, since much taxation and many benefits are matters for the sovereign nations.

Let us suppose that the electorate approves of two principles:

1. No local authority in the UK should have an average living standard lower than 98.5% of the UK mean, expressed in inflation-adjusted (i.e. real) GDP per capita, and

2. After twenty years, the target mean living standard should be reduced from 98.5% to 98% of the UK average.

A formula like this prevents extreme inequality while providing an incentive to the nations to compete to better their economies. It only affects households indirectly.

All that is needed is for the Office for National Statistics to report mid-year population and annual GDP early in the next calendar year, and the transfers for the period beginning 1 April can be calculated.

INTERNATIONAL AGREEMENTS

These are a part of foreign affairs, but there is a situation in which nations (but not regions) may wish to forge their own agreements. A nation may wish to enter into different trade and professional agreements as part of its economic development. The European single market causes a border for application of product, food safety, and veterinary standards, which has been largely resolved in the case of Northern Ireland. Any of the sovereign nations could do the same. The remaining technical barrier is that World Trade Organisation rules require a customs border where trade agreements include tariff rate quotas, that is, tariffs that vary with the volume of goods. Such agreements have to be at the UK level. Other agreements may not require a customs border, although the issue of product equivalence with the single market would remain.

ARTIFICIAL INTELLIGENCE AND THE TECH INDUSTRIES

The big tech companies have gradually morphed into providers of critical infrastructure. They claim to compete but, in reality, they are mostly duopolies, in some cases monopolies competing with very different businesses (for example, online shopping versus the high street). They should be regulated as utilities. Modern life is impossible without their services.

AI demonstrates the classic conflict between freedom to develop and exploit new business ideas and individual rights. The EU puts citizens' rights first; Britain has moved towards a free-for-all.

Two completely different uses of AI have emerged:

1. Judgement use. In this use, the AI system makes decisions, or advises someone what decision to make. This is an evolution from 'Computer knows best', which has always been a concern, even more so since the revelation that English law presumes that systems are free of bugs. AI does not know right from wrong. It has no moral compass. Decision-making affecting outcomes needs audit for accuracy, and I include some suggestions for this in the draft constitution.

2. Efficiency use. This use of AI is an extension of systems improvements, automating tasks that include a degree of selection that earlier systems could not achieve. So long as practical outcomes are not affected and citizens' rights are protected, it is less concerning.

WHAT ELSE?

One reform that I think would best be postponed, is the separation of elections to governments from elections to parliaments. Britain draws its governments from parliaments, both in the present House of Commons and the devolved legislatures. Some other democracies, notably America and Switzerland, separate the two. America elects a president who chooses his cabinet for confirmation by the Senate.

For Britain, the immediate priorities are to make the people's voice heard, end the absolute power of the State, and adopt a federal structure. Separating governments and their parliaments could come later, through the constitutional change process.

5 THE PEOPLE'S COUNCIL

FUNCTIONS OF THE PEOPLE'S COUNCIL

The People's Council should have eight major functions:

1. It should be responsible for ensuring the independence of British institutions, so that they cannot be manipulated by ephemeral political fashions.
2. It should enforce high standards in government, local authorities, all state agencies, regulators, committees, arms-length bodies, and politics, with appropriate power to investigate.
3. It should act as a clearing house for requests from the public for referenda and changes to the constitution, giving the people the right to examine issues and force those issues onto a democratic agenda.
4. It should provide a channel to ensure that the public voice is heard and listened to.
5. It should act as the final arbiter on all legislation.

6. It should provide independent supervision of ombudspersons investigating arbitrary and unfair government acts.

7. It should also provide independent supervision of a straightforward facts hub for reference that the public can understand and rely on[81].

8. It will be able to refer matters to the Constitutional Court.

These functions are much broader than the present non-legislative functions of the House of Commons. The House of Commons has the main function of approving government legislation with little scrutiny and negligible change. It has a secondary function: to reject amendments made by the House of Lords (other than those promoted by the government to fix its own mistakes). The Commons has two other democratic functions, which would better be separated from approving legislation:

1. To scrutinise the conduct of government. Scrutiny of government is poor owing to the power of the party whips. This is a major defect of the present system of political governance. Committee reports are diligently produced, then nothing may happen.

2. To resolve state failures affecting the individual. This belongs in a proper ombudsperson service with authority to require changes, not in a once-a-week question session, which is more concerned with posturing for the media than constraining state power. Such questions are just the visible tip of a large iceberg, whereby government departments may sometimes take months to answer enquiries from MPs.

Organisations forming the British State

The British State has numerous committees, commissions, departments, agencies, arms-length bodies, and public bodies with a variety of powers. There is a list on the gov.uk website[82] which, with references to other public bodies and agencies, runs to 1,022 organisations. Some style themselves as 'Independent' but how many are really serving the people rather than political masters? Here are four examples of variations of independence and political control:

1. Some, such as the Judicial Appointments Commission, are required to be independent by legislation[83].

2. Others – the House of Lords Appointments Commission comes to mind – can only make recommendations to the prime minister; such bodies are not independent of political influence.

3. 'Soft power' has been used to reduce the scope for BBC reporters to challenge government. The government has control of appointments of the chair and non-executive board members; the BBC board appoints the deputy chair and director-general, and the BBC itself selects four executive members, one for each of the four nations. The BBC has an independence objective in its Charter[84], but can be subtly influenced by appointment of the chair and non-executive directors.

4. We noted in the previous chapter that the government of Gibraltar is subject to control from London through the Privy Council.

In these examples, we can see the variations of 'independence': statutory (judicial appointments), meaningless (House of Lords Appointments Commission), possibility of being influenced (the BBC) and misrepresented as to its independence (Gibraltar). It is worth noting that independence of the Judicial Appointments Commission is enshrined in legislation, whereas the toothlessness of the House of

Lords Appointments Commission and the colonial status of Gibraltar both derive from Orders in Council. These are an utterly undemocratic way of making law used by autocratic government to bypass parliament completely.

The People's Council would be able to establish whether any organ of the State – any organisation, institution, agency, committee, or body, including arms-length bodies – is independent. This would be the case if all appointments at senior level were made on merit with no influence from any politician or right to intervene by any government. In this test, of our four examples, only the Judicial Appointments Commission would now be classed as independent. The People's Council should have power to investigate and publish its assessment of whether any organ is truly independent. An organ that is classed as 'not independent' may reform and ask for a reassessment. An organ that is classed as 'independent' should be audited afresh every twenty years, or earlier at public request. All quasi-judicial bodies such as tribunals should be completely independent[85].

Truthfulness and standards

Standards in public life have been debased and twisted. Lies and misinformation became the norm during the 2016 referendum. I said earlier that the UK requires its financial services industry to publish advertisements that are clear, fair, and not misleading. Why not apply the same standard to its politicians, governments, and opinion formers in the media? Adopting the financial services model, every political and government communication and every media report and opinion piece should be approved that it meets this standard by a responsible person with records kept and penalties for non-compliance. This would reduce lies and disinformation.

The People's Council would act as a first-line defence against political lies, media manipulation of the public, and character assassination, receiving complaints from the public and ensuring that dubious claims are corrected and not repeated. There should be a requirement for equal prominence and prompt response, so that false claims can be corrected with the same level of attention, particularly before voting. At present, media corrections to headlines may be in very small print on an inside page six months after a front-page headline. An opinion article read by hundreds of thousands referring, for example, to "Britain's out of control welfare state" would need to cite evidence that either welfare benefits are significantly higher in Britain, or that many more claimants gain benefits than in other similar countries. Facts, not fiction.

High standards are also needed for the behaviour of office holders. Ethics investigations, standards watchdogs, and parliamentary committees should all be supervised by the People's Council. However, an important difference from the present arrangements would be that the People's Council could choose what to investigate and how. It would write its own terms of reference to prevent autocratic control over scope. This would satisfy public concerns.

Standards also apply to governments. They must deal quickly with all services for which they are a monopoly provider. If they require an application from a citizen and it is defective in some way (for example, driving licence and passport provision) they should promptly inform the citizen of what options there are to remedy it. The People's Council should have the power to investigate any government department and the communications of any political party, to ensure that they are keeping to the highest standards.

The power to investigate needs to extend to government agencies, arms-length bodies, and private-sector providers of monopoly essential services. The People's Council should be able to investigate financial engineering and rent-extraction, as they arise, and require changes in the interest of the people. Some owners of English water companies appear to have achieved a similar financial benefit as that of banks before the credit crunch: take excess returns in the good times and either leave the State to bail them out later, or increase charges to correct past underinvestment and over-compensation of owners.

The People's Council would refer any suspicion of criminal behaviour (including corruption) to the police for priority investigation. Ethics, parliamentary, regulatory, and ministerial code failures would be referred to the appropriate authorities, provided they have been vetted as independent; otherwise, the People's Council would carry out its own investigation. Suspicions of major errors affecting many people do occasionally arise; in extreme cases, the People's Council should be able to require the appropriate government to conduct a formal inquiry. No longer will uncomfortable matters be swept under the carpet.

Requests for referenda

There should be a simple method for the public to force issues onto the political agenda. The simplest would be for any campaigning group to submit a proposed referendum, whether at UK, national, regional, or local level. The People's Council can then merge similar demands, ensure that they are practical and sensible, and require the appropriate government to arrange the referendum within a reasonable time: say six months for local, one year for national and two years for UK-wide issues. A threshold level of support would be needed, in the same way that recall elections need sufficient support. The People's Council should also be able to defer silly, trivial, and extremist requests for referenda. However, national, regional, and local referenda may only happen where the sovereign national parliaments allow them.

The People's Council would act as a clearing house for proposed constitutional amendments.

Listening to the people

A simple, fast, efficient way of catching complaints about errors and complaints about governments that do not need legislative change is also needed. Isolated incidents that are personal belong to the ombudsperson services, but general warnings that something is amiss should be identified by the People's Council. For example, multiple complaints about a failing or misguided government policy and multiple complaints about a monopoly public service may indicate something that needs attention. The State should respond promptly, efficiently, and with accuracy rather than spin.

Assent to legislation

Royal assent is meaningless. The King does what the UK government says, even to the extent of refusing assent for legislation passed by national parliaments. Royal assent should be replaced by the people's assent.

However, not everything needs to come before the People's Council. If the people have clearly understood and voted to accept a political proposal, including a statement of intent setting out the objectives and direction of the proposed legislation, then no further ratification should be needed. The People's Council would get involved where there is no clear mandate, as a check to prevent unclear alternatives or undemocratic legislation.

Ombudspersons

There should be a public ombudsperson service for all governments including local governments, supervised by the People's Council, with authority to require changes. These ombudspersons may be part-time but must be supervised to ensure that the State never uses its might to crush an individual.

The facts hub

Opposing the absolute power of autocrats also needs accurate and easily available facts. National Statistics do excellent work in establishing facts, but far too often the detail is lost in vast indecipherable spreadsheets and may be obscured by political spin in government announcements. Who better than the People's Council to supervise a facts hub[81]?

Referrals to the Constitutional Court

This Court is defined in Chapter 8. The People's Council will have the right to refer matters to the Court. It will also examine all other Court applications and report on their merits on behalf of the people, for the Court to consider.

LEGISLATIVE MANDATES AND VENUES

The concept of the electoral mandate has been grossly abused. Governments now force any policy they like through parliament, irrespective of whether the electorate has agreed to it or not. At present the Scottish, Welsh, and Northern Irish legislatures are unicameral, with only Royal assent as a theoretical check. The House of Lords has a meaningless revising function that can be overridden by the government of the day, but this revising function only applies to UK-wide legislation and to all legislation specific to England, with restrictions on 'money bills'. Since all nations should be equal, all national parliaments have the same authority, and more time will be available to get legislation right first time, the Lords has no purpose.

As the Commons would also become five parliaments (one federal and four national, of which three already exist), the palace of Westminster would be redundant. Its use could be changed, perhaps to a tourist attraction, although Westminster Hall should be retained for state and other occasions. Instead of spending £6 billion (and rising) on refurbishment as a working centre of autocratic control, why not change its status from a royal palace exempt from all normal building and use controls, and let a developer exploit it for public benefit, albeit subject to UNESCO world heritage constraints? The only alternative is to ask the people to choose, by referendum, between such a project and keeping the English parliament in unsuitable premises in London at vast expense, preserving the ancient dividing lines and antagonisms[86].

Creation of the People's Council removes the need for bicameral parliaments, since there will be effective checks on poor legislation, whereas the current system of a bicameral parliament followed by Royal assent is neutered by the governing party's whips. However, England may still feel attached to an additional toothless talking-shop. Nothing in my draft constitution prevents England from choosing to keep the House of Lords, for England alone.

The people's assent

Here is how this would work. Every party aspiring to form a government, whether of one of the nations, or of the UK, may publish an election manifesto, but meaningless words will be banned. A manifesto needs to state the clear direction of policy. Thus "Get Brexit done" would have been invalid, whereas "Leave the EU, single market and customs union with a trade agreement" would have been valid. "Review rights" would be invalid but "Restrict voting and demonstration rights" would be valid. Anything requiring international negotiation needs specific possible outcomes to be defined.

In the case of domestic legislation, either at UK or national level, there would also need to be a clear statement of policy and its intentions published with the manifesto. The manifesto and policy statement together would be a *potential* basis for an electoral mandate. Actual legislation that keeps closely to the stated intent, or less-significant international agreements that keep closely to the promises made, would be considered as approved by the people.

Why is this combination a *potential* basis? Because the various policies contained in a manifesto need to be unbundled. At present voters have to choose all the policies in a manifesto, even if they reject some. This is not democratic.

Any other legislation or international agreement (including all trade agreements) would require explicit consent by the people. In non-controversial cases, this can be given by vote in the People's Council. Anything else should be approved by the people in a referendum on the actual legislation. Negotiators of international agreements would be given added strength by being able to say, "We could never get that concession through the People's Council." Back-of-the-envelope concessions at dinner, relying on Crown prerogative, will no longer be possible.

CHOOSING AND REFRESHING THE PEOPLE'S COUNCIL

A diverse range of abilities and skills will be needed: interview skills, data analysis, subject knowledge, community involvement. However, long-term career tenure is not appropriate. Membership terms need to be long enough to build and then transfer experience and knowledge, but not so long that entrenched positions become established. For a young person, a few years working in the People's Council should be a desirable career move. They would serve the people, rather than promote ideology, which is the purpose of today's special advisers. Good people need to come forward, particularly for leadership roles, and a demographic balance should be maintained.

Political activities are incompatible with an independent standard-setting body. The various legislatures are political; the People's Council must be apolitical. Former politicians (from both Houses of Parliament and also local authorities) are welcome for their expertise but will need to withdraw from political activity while they serve on the People's Council. They will also need a period of several years out of political representation to appreciate the normal pressures faced by the public, akin to the two-year moratorium on former cabinet ministers taking private-sector employment. Perhaps there could be a credit for full-time employment in a charity working with people experiencing homelessness and/or having been dispossessed, asylum seekers and refugees, or people living in poverty.

Here we come to a fundamental choice: should the People's Council be elected, appointed, or chosen by lot? An elected body will have democratic legitimacy, although it would need structuring to ensure skills, quality, and leadership. An appointed body would have far less credibility, just like the House of Lords, so I will not consider it.

The third alternative is interesting: Athenian democracy was based on citizens chosen by lot (called 'Sortition' by academics)[87]. Random selection has been refined over the centuries to work well for criminal and coroner's juries and is used to create citizen juries to debate policy in a number of countries. Citizen juries are an option for Britain and have been used by academics. Selection by lot has worked elsewhere. The People's Council needs skills and leadership which may be uncertain using selection by lot. But it also needs all parts of society to be represented, including those whose lives have been made miserable by the many policy failures of the past forty years: for example, students, carers, the unemployed, the chronically ill, those experiencing homelessness and/or destitution, and families struggling with mortgages. We assume today that democracy requires elections, but random selection is equally democratic.

The People's Council would need to stay in touch with those it represents and, at the same time, keep apart from populist pressure. My democratic concept is to use two separate groups of elected members, by regulated professions and all others, and within each group to have a leadership candidate list and a general membership list. In addition to this, there should be a third group of citizens chosen by sortition, to ensure that all parts of society are represented. This would numerically be taken from the general group so that only the selection method differs: a form of extended jury service for society.

The points that follow are designed to achieve this. All groups are separate by nation; the UK functions of the People's Council will be met by the groups working together.

1. *The regulated group*

There are 199 UK regulated professions[88]. All these have statutory agencies or private-sector bodies granting licences to practice. Therefore they should have ethical and moral standards and (albeit varied) enforcement procedures. Any person authorised by one of these bodies should be able to vote for candidates standing from the membership of those professions. As a rough estimate, there may be six or seven million people thus qualified to vote. They could vote for 76 positions on the People's Council, allocated to the four nations 8:13:21:34, with some additional places for the overseas territories.

2. *The general group*

All other electors should vote by nation for a general group of candidates. This may include some with previous legislative experience (although they will need to step down from political party membership if elected) and civil society leaders. Professions not included in the regulated group, including many academics (i.e. excluding those qualified for the regulated group), should be able to stand for the general group. There is a vast pool of people who would make good candidates, including early and recent retirees and younger people seeking to broaden their experience. The national membership here could be 34:55:89:144, again with additional overseas territory members, so that the total membership of the People's Council would be just over 400. In the first three years, the general group could be smaller (perhaps 21:34:55:89) so that experience can be built.

3. The sortition group
This small group should be chosen by the national governments from poorly represented demographics, by lot. They would form part of the general group, and their number would be deducted from the number of elected general group members for that nation. The detail of how this could be made to work is in Article 107 of the draft Constitution.

Figure 2 (opposite) maps the groups in the People's Council to its responsibilities.

Leadership, building expertise, teamwork
In each election, there should be two lists. One, for one, two, three or five members within the regulated group and two, three, five or eight members within the general group (according to nation), should be for a leadership team. Leadership candidates may also stand for the main membership. All the remaining places are for the main membership elected from the second list in each group. Every voter will have three votes, one for the leadership list and two for the main membership.

The leadership team would be formed at national level from the elected leaders of both regulated and general groups, and at UK level (for when the People's Council considers UK-wide matters) from all elected leaders. It would be responsible for planning initial workload and assigning members to topics and tasks, taking account of their interests, skills and abilities. Some tasks would be naturally suited to home working with regular meetings and support, while others may require travelling. Members should work in teams; each should probably be of three, five or seven members, always including some members from the professional group.

The general group should provide a range of career opportunities for younger people. It is also desirable for some members of the general group to be part-time to enable a wide range of community and civil society involvement. All members who are not retired should be given employment release and their employers compensated for pay and on-

The People's Council

	Regulated professions	General group	Sortition group
Elected/chosen by lot	Elected by members of regulated professions	Elected by all other voters	Chosen by ballot from under-represented demographics
	Two lists, leadership, 1 vote and members, 2 votes	*Two lists, leadership, 1 vote and members, 2 votes*	*Selected by national governments*
Term of office	Four years (renewable once)	Three years (renewable twice)	One term of three years
Numbers (NI: Wales: Scotland: England)	*8: 12: 21: 34*	*21: 34: 55: 89 at first, then 34: 55: 89: 144*	*3: 5: 8: 13 taken from general group, optional*
Verify independent institutions	✓	✓	✓
Verify high standards (and investigations)	✓	✓	✓
Referendums and constitutional changes	✓	✓	✓
Hearing public concerns	✓	✓	✓
People's assent to legislation	✓	✓	✓
Supervise ombudspersons	✓	✓	✓
Supervise facts hub	✓	✓	✓
Referrals to Court	✓	✓	✓

Figure 2: The People's Council

costs (with appropriate arrangements for the self-employed). Retired and non-working members should be given an honorarium.

The People's Council has both to maintain expertise and continually refresh itself. Those members elected from professions should serve a four-year term renewable once; all others should serve a three-year term renewable twice, with discontinuous membership allowed to both groups. Members standing for re-election may move between the ordinary members and leadership and vice versa.

The People's Council would do some of the work of exercising proper democratic control rather than letting an elite govern as it likes. Cost savings from abolishing both the Privy Council and House of Lords would offset its own costs. It may need to draw on expert advice, either as remunerated technical advisers to smaller investigations, or as experts to contribute to major ones of considerable public concern. However, this is not a formal judicial body: all cases that belong to the judiciary, coroners, or tribunals will be passed to them.

Citizens themselves would become more involved in governance. Many now only pay attention when there is an election. Reinventing democracy also brings responsibilities for every citizen, to inform themselves about issues sufficiently to vote. It also brings responsibilities for governments, to ensure that all views are properly advised to citizens without bias, emotion, or spin. We need to return to the days when political governance included leadership of the people via education and explanation, in lieu of the puerile attacks and false dividing lines that set citizen against citizen. According to Robert Peston, honest, rational discourse should replace misinformation and evasion of questions[89].

6 THE NEW GOVERNMENTS

LEVELS OF GOVERNANCE AND OVERSIGHT

Government fit for the twenty-first century and beyond needs to locate powers at the most sensible level, even if it means allowing some change from the 'one-size-fits-all' nature of centralised control. Local economies differ, and effective governments would combine all viewpoints including those of business and universities. Working together is always more productive than any alternative[90].

Here are the possible levels of governance and oversight:

UK responsibilities

Defence, foreign affairs, the currency, the sovereign grant, and, to the extent provided here, international agreements including trade agreements requiring borders, common services and minimum standards for pensions, and all technical standards requiring consistency such as international financial requirements, roads, railways, air travel, and tourist visas.

UK Government
Defence, foreign affairs, common standards

Scotland, Wales, and Northern Ireland
All other policy areas

England
Social policy, elections, infrastructure

English regions
Health, education, transport, employment, housing, planning, business, industry, and work visas

Local authorities
Existing structure and responsibilities

Figure 3: Governments, if England adopts regions

UK Government
Defence, foreign affairs, common standards

England, Scotland, Wales, and Northern Ireland
All other policy areas

Local authorities
Existing structure and responsibilities

Figure 4: Governments, if England rejects regions

England, Scotland, Wales, Northern Ireland, and overseas territories

Healthcare, education, transport, employment, housing, social care, old age, disability, child support, asylum, elections, the environment, and all other economic powers (i.e. planning, business and industry, and work visas). Within Great Britain and Northern Ireland, the nations should be free to negotiate international agreements that enhance their trade and prosperity but do not require internal borders: in effect, this allows some mutual recognition of standards but prohibits all agreements that set or affect customs tariffs. The overseas territories can continue with existing arrangements at their democratic determination.

Regions

If the people of England agree, health, education, transport, employment, housing, planning, business, industry, and work visas may be transferred to regional governments supervised by a regional parliament. At a later date, Scotland and Wales may also wish to consider regional governance. However, some infrastructure planning such as water, power, major roads and railways, and some resilience planning would need national-level coordination. Compromise and consensus become more important once central control is eliminated.

The functions of governments (with and without English regions) are shown in Figures 3 and 4 (see previous pages).

THE NEED FOR CHANGE

The concepts in the chapters that follow are purely to start the discussion, since nobody has faced the need for a federal structure. Only those powers that need to be central should be central. Everything else belongs to the sovereign nations. Regional governments would enable the regions to prosper, particularly in England.

The monarchy can be privileged and on a pedestal, which brings in tourist revenue but it should be completely outside politics. It is a solid institution that works hard, albeit with occasional mistakes. The people must decide which they prefer: equality or privilege. This book suggests a path for the people to choose, while separating the Crown from its present role deeply embedded into political governance.

Replacing Crown prerogative is key to this change. Crown prerogative is anti-democratic, since it allows government to do as it likes, notably when negotiating international agreements.

Crown privilege is different. It says the monarchy is above the law. While nobody can be too concerned about a few Royal cars having no license plates, there are more troublesome aspects to this. Parliament sits in a Royal palace, which takes it outside the scope of legislation. Therefore, MPs and Lords do not pay any duties on alcohol bought on the parliamentary estate. Normal health, safety, and employment rules do not apply[58]. In my view, this is one of the causes of the 'one rule for them and another for us' mentality. Another aspect is that it is impossible to treat everyone as equal before the law, because all those who live and work in Royal palaces are to some extent above the law.

Nonetheless, the monarchy does have a function. It provides continuity for the important role of head of state. The question to be addressed is this: do the political compromises of the seventeenth century, whereby the monarchy retained political involvement through the Privy Council, Crown prerogative, privilege, and immunity, all remain appropriate in the twenty-first century?

REVENUE AND BORROWING

From where should our new governments get their revenue? There are three broad choices: taxes, borrowing, and user fees for services, supplemented or reduced by transfers. The principles of a cash transfer mechanism were discussed in Chapter 4. Both the UK government and national governments would be taxing authorities. Proposed taxes must be clear at the outset, as otherwise people will assume that they will rise.

UK government revenue

There is one tax that should obviously be UK wide: value added tax (VAT). For if it is not uniform, evasion will be caused by movement between the nations. Luckily VAT raises about twice the defence budget, and defence will be the second biggest UK government expense. The much smaller revenues from customs and excise duties and withholding taxes would be simpler if administered and collected centrally.

Revenues of England, Scotland, Wales, and Northern Ireland

The sovereign nations (and, of course, the overseas territories) would be free to choose what taxes they wish to levy and how to levy them. Income and capital gains taxes become a national responsibility, not federal, so the nations set their levels and rules and retain the revenue.

The nations would also decide how to fund their regional and local governments. Council tax and business rates could be replaced in an enterprising nation by local income and company taxes as an uplift to any national taxes. Your author pays separate municipal, cantonal, and federal income taxes; the overall level is lower than in the UK.

Revenue sources for the regions

Regional governments, if formed, would be funded either by local taxes or by cash transfers from national governments, perhaps both. Healthcare costs are high, and regions would need financial support from national government revenue.

Government borrowing

Government borrowing could be left to the UK government, rather than force national governments to incur higher interest rates by arranging their own borrowing. Interest costs would leave a deficit, although they may be recharged to the nations eventually (if approved by the people, of course). If existing interest costs are not recharged to the nations, then the transfer mechanism might need to operate in reverse, with the nations using a tiny part of their taxation revenue to fund the UK government. This can be seen in these figures, which are approximate estimates for 2023[91]:

Interest cost of debt	£110bn
Defence budget	+ £55bn
Outlay on major items	**£165bn**
VAT revenue	£162bn

But there is a case for each national government to create its own credit record over time by arranging its own new borrowing. This is a matter for debate and vote.

Treasury accounts include both capital and current expenditure, and the misleading practice has grown of defining all expenditure as investment. Capital and current expenditures need to be clearly separated so that all government accounts at every level show borrowing to fund capital expenditure separately from any day-to-day deficits. Spending is not all investment, despite the definitions used by past chancellors.

It would also be necessary to distinguish inherited debt (the total national debt when the constitution comes into effect) from new borrowing. New borrowing would need to be negotiated between the governments, ideally in proportion to desired public capital investment. The interest costs of new borrowing should belong to the government raising money to fund capital investment.

User fees

Many government services are funded by user fees: think passports and driving licences for obvious examples. User fees should be reasonable for the service provided, and service provision should be prompt.

There should be no overcharging of captive users of monopoly services. Apart from the special conditions associated with 'settled status' for free-movement nationals permanently resident in the UK, other non-citizens who are permanently resident have to pay both visa fees and a health surcharge, renewable every five years. This is double taxation of those working and contributing to British society. It creates a financial disincentive to recruitment from abroad. The fees charged are high by international standards, amounting to exploitation of those with no vote.

Tourist visas (including short-term working visits) belong at the UK level. Work visas giving permanent residence rights are a matter for the nations and, where they exist, regions. Work visas are ripe for competition between nations and regions.

Wealth taxes

Wealth taxes should belong to the sovereign nations, but here again they may compete by designing taxes other than inheritance tax, which as it stands is easily avoided.

PENSIONS, HEALTHCARE COSTS, AND SOCIAL SECURITY

Minimum standards should be set by the UK parliament for state pensions. The sovereign nations and regions should be free to exceed the minima. The people should be asked whether they wish to change from a pay-as-you-go pension system to a funded system; the latter would have to be built up slowly over at least half a century.

Britain has relatively poor state pensions (even with the rises in recent years) offset for some by occupational schemes. Those occupational schemes providing pension guarantees are largely mature, have low levels of new membership, and need to invest cautiously to meet their obligations. Government would like them to provide the funds for its schemes, rather than raise taxes or public borrowing. Such pension funds should not be subject to unnecessary risks. As for defined contribution schemes without pension guarantees, they could offer a public project investment fund and see how much capital they can raise. But government should not be demanding that future and current pensioners provide its risk capital.

Britain needs a serious debate about taxation levels and public services. Allowing nations to compete would open up the possibility of change. Some European countries use insured healthcare, with restrictions on medical underwriting, so that those with ill-health do not incur any penalty. An enterprising nation could design such a system for its healthcare and take the proposal to the people. Lower taxes and shorter waiting lists would follow, but the individual would pay insurance premiums (reimbursed for those living in poverty and those with disabilities). Each nation could develop its own proposals. **This is sovereignty.**

Social security benefits and funding should probably belong to the nations. There is a case to be made for minimum standards, but equally there is a case for national variations. When in doubt, the sovereignty of the nations ought to prevail.

OTHER CHANGES THAT ARE NEEDED

Centralised policies never satisfy everyone. They produce statist solutions in which a cult of uniformity develops. One element of the change that is needed is to allow the smaller nations and the English regions to develop their own solutions for economic growth, based on their natural resources, infrastructure, and human potential.

The intense pressures and shortage of time under centralised government lead to poor decisions and poor legislation. It would be much better to have more people involved in political governance and many more points of view. National sovereignty with multiple parliaments clears the way for more part-time involvement. At present, part-time involvement is restricted to those able to exploit connections with large businesses and a lucky few professionals who practise in and around London.

What is needed is for local government to develop its own leadership around what is good for the nation or region. Having their own taxation and spending powers (plus financial adjustment of resources by cash transfers) would enable nations and regions to flourish.

Localism also allows coordination of state services. Instead of the citizen handling a variety of state agencies in their vertical silos (health, education, benefits, employment, and housing are examples); the citizen can be placed at the centre of coordinated action.

In England, the development of mayors provides a nucleus to commence formation of some regions. There is a snag: they will mainly be based around cities or existing conurbations. It may be necessary to allow rural areas, which have different needs from cities, to form regions and thereby participate in national and inter-regional cash transfers.

These are structural changes, but another deep failure hit me when I read the Australian constitution. This was originally an Act of the UK parliament, consisting of enabling clauses that transferred colonies to independent states with a constitution included in the text of the Act. It is a nightmare of legal complexity, full of 'notwithstanding' clauses and lengthy sentences with so many subordinate clauses that it is difficult for the reader to comprehend. The earlier Canadian constitution is similar, but a major amendment in 1982 is somewhat easier to follow and more oriented to the people.

The German, Italian and Swiss constitutions are completely different[92]. Instead of being stuffed full of indecipherable legalese, they all clearly put the citizen first. The people matter. This shows two other facets of Britain's political obsession with the seventeenth century. One is that state power is absolute, and people count for little. At the policy-making level, state interests come first, second and third, and Britain seems to easily find loopholes asserting state power[93], while, at the other extreme, petty bureaucrats are given licence to treat those at the bottom of the heap with contempt.

Political governance needs to be designed for the future, not the past. It really is time to put the absolute power of the seventeenth century, with two gladiators fighting for turns at forcing any laws they like through parliament, out to grass. The model of government based on courtiers fighting for the ear of an absolute ruler, revealed by the Covid enquiry, should go.

People must be treated decently. Policies need unbundling. The constitution must be an easily understood document. Power must come from the people, not the State. Then Britain will have a chance of coping with the complexity of the twenty-first century. The alternative? Continued decline and eventual break-up of the UK.

7 HOW CHANGE COULD BE ACHIEVED

It is possible, but I fear unlikely, that one of the main political parties will consider these ideas. Without such a sponsor, how can the people extricate Britain from its present mess? Britain will never escape its repetitive failures unless the people demand change. Therefore, tell the politicians at every opportunity that you want constitutional reform.

There will be severe resistance from vested interests. In the University College London conference that I referred to earlier[76], Lord Falconer said that only a determined leader with a large majority in the Commons could pursue constitutional reform. The House itself would object to weakening the ability of a Prime Minister to bestow patronage. How revealing! This example of an establishment figure defending the status quo shows why the people must demand change, so that a new leader grasps the potential and makes an electoral case for the Commons to surrender the benefits of patronage handed out by the powerful. Again, we come back to the solution of nearly four centuries ago dictating our twenty-first century governance. Apart from women's emancipation and the Great Reform Act, there is little evidence that the people have much more power today than at the restoration of the monarchy in 1660.

However, I disagree with Lord Falconer that a large majority is a necessary precondition for substantial reform. A hung parliament is unpredictable. The 2017 parliament was manipulated by the European Research Group (whose knowledge of Europe could possibly have been better researched) because a small group seized a chance to control the government. A hung parliament arising out of public disaffection with our political system might just be open to a deal between several smaller parties and more thoughtful large party backbenchers to avoid a further election by insisting on policies that the party leaders would rather avoid. It all depends on how strongly the people say "We want democratic reform instead of this slide to autocracy." Until the people drag Britain out of the seventeenth century, nothing will change. Adopting the concepts in this book would be one way a future government could serve the people.

The national priority is to run two major change projects at once. This is the only way to reverse the damage of multiple failed policies that culminated in the UK imposing trade sanctions on itself. This book sets out one project; the other is, to quote Professor Andrew Blick, to "get Brexit undone"[94]. Complaining about the cost of living, lack of doctor's appointments, and inflation is to focus on symptoms, not causes. When you focus on symptoms, politicians can offer palliatives that will never solve the underlying problems. The NHS workforce plan, for example, assumes there will be ample senior doctors to train increasing numbers of medical students, which is unrealistic given the growing waiting lists.

Only focus on the root causes will drag Britain out of its malaise. The causes are the series of failed policies discussed in Chapter 2, all made possible by the weakness of British democracy. Britain is now in a trap of its own making, in which trade with Europe continues to decline, so tax revenues fall, leading to worse services and further deterioration of infrastructure. In turn this results in reduced investment in Britain, fewer jobs, higher prices in shops from import barriers, further deterioration of trade, and higher taxes. It's a vicious circle from which the only escape will be to get much closer to Europe.

Rejoining the customs union would remove all bureaucracy that has throttled business, dispose of awful trade agreements that will damage British farming for little or no net gain, and (with single market membership) remove the last checks in the Irish Sea. But note that, in order to make the rules, Britain would need to accept that "Brussels rules" was a lie and rejoin the European Union, shorn of some of its previous membership concessions. There is no good compromise.

How, then, could Britain embrace both federalism and some element of direct democracy so as to give its people a much greater democratic stake in solving the mess many generations of politicians have brought about? How can it put a stop to the lies and disinformation that have brought Britain so low? I would suggest there are stages to go through, that collectively would take about seventeen years.

The first step will be exhaustive discussion of the concepts in this book, recognising that they are ideas for development, rather than a prescribed solution. The whole concept needs approval by the people. Here's how it could be developed.

There should be a series of referenda at a national level, requiring a majority of the nations to agree, but slight differences in wording will be needed as follows. All four referenda should be held at the same time, and England must not use its numbers as a blocking vote.

England

The preliminary referendum question could be:

> "Should the UK adopt a written federal constitution, in which all nations are equal, and, if so, do you agree that England should not be able to use its numerical majority of about 84% of the total population to overrule the other nations?"

Expect the Establishment to find every reason why England should vote No.

Scotland and Wales

In these two nations the questions are identical:

> "Should the UK adopt a written federal constitution, in which all nations are equal and England cannot impose its numerical majority on the other nations?"

Northern Ireland

A written constitution will need to provide for the unique issues affecting Northern Ireland:

> "Should the UK adopt a written federal constitution, in which all nations are equal and England cannot impose its numerical majority on the other nations, while protecting the 1998 Belfast Agreement and the ability of the people of Northern Ireland to make amendments thereto?"

INTERPRETATION OF PRELIMINARY RESULTS

For the project to go ahead, any three out of the four nations comprising Great Britain and Northern Ireland need to vote "Yes", and there needs to be a majority of the total votes (and possibly, at least 50% of the electorate voting "Yes"). For perhaps the first time ever, England could be overruled by the three other nations acting together. All four nations would be equal.

If the people vote in favour of federalism and some direct democracy in principle, then England should vote, again in principle, on whether it wants to be unitary or regional. Again, this would take a year or two to set out a coherent proposition and get it through parliament.

If this second stage gains the people's approval for English regional government, then detailed proposals would be needed, which would take time to draw up. Further referenda should follow to ensure this process delivers something acceptable to the majority.

This is the point at which a constitutional convention becomes advisable. The people have spoken and said they desire significant change; the Establishment and the two main parties must accept that they will lose absolute power. The UK will have a future beyond managed decline.

Finally, in the fourth stage, implementation can be planned. The result, probably ten to fifteen years down the road, will be the end of Britain's centralised government, excepting defence, foreign affairs, trade policy, and the currency. Those are the common responsibilities of federal governments in the nations we have studied. Overall, there would be a peaceful way to enable Britain to face up to its debt burden, climate change, and the impact of both on people, rather than drifting towards riots, insurrection, or breaking up.

Local initiative would be needed to get the ball rolling on regional government in England. The centre will never volunteer to reduce its power. Regional English parliaments could be proposed by at least two first-tier local authorities acting together. The other nations may adopt regions subsequently. Since it is not possible to presume what the people may say in the earlier stages, the issue of the scope of an English parliament versus regional parliaments cannot be designed now. This depends on whether regions are adopted, and their scale.

I put forward a draft constitution in this book as a way of commencing debate. For without it, the whole project could be abandoned. This draft needs to be taken as just that: a first draft. It needs extensive work before it can go to the people for their approval. Hopefully some of the academics whose views I have discussed will grasp the issue.

ADOPTING THE NEW CONSTITUTION

The people should have a choice of voting entirely "Yes" or "No" or voting article by article and even line by line, to express dissent from specific items. Voting would therefore need to be spread over several days. Perhaps instead of sending polling cards to electors, they could be sent the draft constitution, each copy with a unique barcode, set out so that electors can vote in principle or in detail on their copy and return it to the town hall or polling station.

There would be a lengthy implementation period. New national and regional governments would have to be built up slowly, and central government run down at the same pace. Whereas Scotland, Wales, and Northern Ireland have a basic infrastructure to start with, England has none, apart from those Whitehall departments whose scope is largely or exclusively English now.

This takes us to the role of the civil service. The late Prof. Anthony King[95] argued that the civil service and Thatcher/Blair governments hollowed out local government, imposing central control. Whitehall operates in functional silos and Britain generally focuses too much on process and not enough on objectives or outcomes, a point that the EU well understood in the Brexit negotiations. Operational cross-departmental work can only improve by adopting federal and regional government. It might even create a happier, contented civil service rather than the unhappy one described by Camilla Cavendish[96]. It is axiomatic that the civil service will become much more decentralised under this new constitution, with the Treasury and Home Office both losing power. One reason why I have allowed so much time for changes is to permit proper plans for the civil service to be drawn up and implemented.

TIMELINE

The timeline is broad because change will only happen when the people demand it, and parliament recognises that change is essential. The people need more understanding of the concepts in this book. The media could conduct investigations of other democratic systems, particularly those that focus on compromise rather than fighting for absolute power.

Here is a possible timeline:

Discussion in the media and education of the people	**One to two years**
Legislation for preliminary referenda	**One to six years**
National referenda held	**Three months**
If approved, England votes for regions or unitary government	**One to two years**
Constitutional convention, detailed proposals	**Three to four years**
Approval referendum and contingency	**Up to three years**

This gives a total of up to seventeen years if the next parliament grasps the issues, longer if it takes two parliaments to get started.

8 FIRST-DRAFT CONSTITUTION OF THE UNITED KINGDOM

NOTES

In order to keep the text of the book brief, not every point in the draft Constitution has been explained in previous chapters. Some of the articles have notes immediately following their text, but many are self-explanatory. There is some deliberate detail in an attempt to prevent the powerful from finding or creating loopholes.

THE DRAFT CONSTITUTION

The British people resolving to renew their unity so as to strengthen liberty, democracy, independence and peace in a spirit of solidarity and openness towards the world,

- determining to live together with mutual consideration and respect for their diversity,

- conscious of their common achievements and their responsibility towards future generations,

- in the knowledge that only those who use their freedom remain free, and that the strength of a people is measured by the well-being of its weakest members,

- and asserting that the State is the servant of the people and not their master,

adopt the following Constitution:

The preamble is taken from the Swiss constitution, with the last point added by this author to emphasise that the era of governments doing as they like, without democratic consent, is over.

1.
    (a) The United Kingdom shall protect the liberty and rights of all the people, and safeguard the independence and security of the country.

    (b) It shall promote the common welfare, sustainable development, internal cohesion, and cultural diversity of the country.

    (c) It shall ensure the greatest possible equality of opportunity among its citizens.

    (d) It is committed to the long-term preservation of natural resources and the environment, and to a just and peaceful international order.

    (e) It shall maintain economic prosperity, while ensuring a decent living standard for the less fortunate.

    (f) It shall engage with the world and re-establish its reputation for democracy and for respecting international law.

(g) It shall provide a worthwhile future for younger generations, eschewing inter-generational unfairness.

2. In this Constitution, the term "State" means any and all units, departments, governments, local authorities, agencies, committees, regulators, arms-length bodies, and any parts thereof as the context may imply:

   (a) All activities of the State are based on and limited by law.

   (b) State activities must be conducted in the public interest and be proportionate to the ends sought.

   (c) The State and private persons shall act in good faith.

   (d) The United Kingdom and the nations shall respect international law, which is superior to this Constitution when made in accordance with this Constitution, and shall respect the Belfast Agreement of 1998 and any amendments to it, which are also superior to this Constitution.

   (e) Where the interests of capital and the people are opposed, a fair balance shall be maintained. If no fair balance is possible, then the interests of the people come first. However, company liquidations shall always allocate liabilities in the order: taxes, social security due, equity, debt securities, suppliers, customers.

3.

   (a) Each of the nations of England, Scotland, Wales, and Northern Ireland is sovereign and makes its own laws in accordance with this Constitution.

   (b) The nations agree that defence, foreign affairs, the currency, the sovereign grant, and, to the extent provided here, international agreements including trade, shall be a collective endeavour for

FIRST-DRAFT CONSTITUTION OF THE UNITED KINGDOM

the good of all participating nations supervised by the United Kingdom parliament.

(c) The nations agree that common services and minimum standards, including financial services commitments, pensions, technical standards, and infrastructure affecting multiple nations, shall be maintained as a United Kingdom facility on the authority of each and every nation.

(d) The nations may enter into agreements with each other that do not conflict with matters reserved to the United Kingdom parliament.

(e) The nations are bound by international law and exercise their own sovereign responsibilities.

(f) The Head of State shall be the Monarch. Succession shall be according to established law. The People's Council together with not more than five representatives of every parliament, and optionally one for each Overseas Territory, shall determine accession.

(g) The Head of State has the prerogative of mercy, to be exercised either on the Head of State's own initiative or on the advice of any government. All other prerogatives are abolished.

(h) The seabed belongs to the people of the nation that it surrounds (with a midline for separation of Northern Ireland and Great Britain), and its wealth belongs equally to both future and present generations.

(i) All government meetings, informal discussions, and communications must be recorded and, save for the most sensitive security and diplomatic issues, available on request by any citizen. State record destruction of any type requires the prior approval of the People's Council.

(j) All parts of the State must make every effort to ensure that lessons learnt are not forgotten but are carried forward to future generations through appropriate management education.

(k) A person shall not be qualified to serve at the most senior levels of any government, whether elected or otherwise, unless holding the qualifications indicated:

Foreign secretary	A spoken foreign language at A2 level or two spoken foreign languages at A1 level or residence as an adult for at least five years in a non-English speaking country
Defence secretary	Two years' service in the armed services or five years as a reservist
A trade minister	At least five years' experience in business, industry, or a profession
A business minister	At least five years' experience in business, industry, or a profession
A finance minister	A degree or professional qualification in economics, finance, accounting, or a postgraduate degree in any broad management discipline
A justice minister	A degree or professional qualification in law
An energy or environment minister	A degree in any scientific discipline
A health minister	A medical qualification or a degree in any biological discipline
A transport minister	At least five years' experience in business, industry, or a profession

(l) Every parliament shall make similar qualification standards for its senior ministers and civil servants.

(m) Each department of the United Kingdom and national governments may appoint one person at public expense to provide political advice to ministers. Such appointments rank as senior civil servants for qualification requirements. No other appointments of political or other advisers are allowed. External part-time departmental directors may be appointed, provided they do not have a political advisory role.

(n) All appointments at director level to any part of the State must be advertised widely, stating the required qualifications. Candidates may only be appointed on merit, which shall be assessed as strategic thinking, a questioning mind, and relevant knowledge.

(o) Any responsibility not defined in this Constitution belongs to the sovereign nations.

Article 3 makes the nations sovereign and defines the responsibilities of the UK government. Although foreign affairs and international agreements are a UK responsibility, the nations must still observe all agreements.

The monarch continues as head of state. This constitution will bring enough changes without starting a debate about the future of the monarchy. The monarchy's non-democratic role in political governance would be reduced.

Article 3 (g) abolishes Crown prerogative but not Crown privilege. Crown prerogative has no place in a twenty-first century democracy. It is a remnant of autocratic Britain, which allows governments to do as they like unless specifically constrained by legislation. Crown privilege overrules the principle that everyone is equal before the law. It is not possible to have both equality before the law and Crown privilege. They are mutually exclusive. This is a matter for a separate referendum which would be possible under this Constitution.

The practice of appointing amateurs with no relevant knowledge to key government positions and as political advisers is ended.

4.

    (a) Where this Constitution is silent, existing law shall prevail.

    (b) This Constitution may only be amended in accordance with its provisions.

    (c) The nations inherit existing laws excepting those matters reserved to the United Kingdom parliament.

    (d) If any part of this Constitution is found by a court to be invalid or contradictory, that shall not affect the remainder of this Constitution.

5.

    (a) Apart from England (which retains a choice), all parliaments of the nations shall be unicameral and formed from their existing parliaments.

    (b) England shall consider what future form of political governance it needs, allowing for reduced national functions if regional parliaments develop.

    (c) All parliaments shall sit in rounded chambers that are at least a semicircle or horseshoe, without dividing lines or other artificial restraints to communication between members. They shall follow standards of considerate discourse and eschew rowdy behaviour.

    (d) The United Kingdom parliament and government shall be located in a city that is not the home of any national parliament, with good transport connections to the entire United Kingdom and internationally, chosen by all the people (see Article 115).

    (e) The Palace of Westminster (excluding Westminster Hall, which shall remain available for state occasions) may be redeveloped as a tourist attraction, with profits and costs shared by all the nations in proportion to population.

If England insists – by vote – on keeping its traditions of political antagonism and a bicameral national parliament, then Article 5 (c) would need amendment and 5 (e) would have to be deleted.

6.

(a) Any region of England may acquire full economic powers if approved by those people directly affected (referred to subsequently as "the relevant people"). A region shall consist of at least two first-tier local authorities with a common boundary. Regions should where possible align with Integrated Care Boards.

(b) All such authorities acting together may initiate formation of a region having no detached parts. Formation must be approved by the relevant people.

(c) No region may be formed that at inception would have a population larger than that of Greater London, unless it consists of an existing Integrated Care Board in its entirety and that arrangement is approved by the relevant people.

(d) The area of an Integrated Care Board may be divided into two or more regions if approved by the relevant people.

(e) Several Integrated Care Boards may form one region if approved by the relevant people.

(f) Full economic powers include health, education, transport, housing, planning, business and industry, and work visas.

(g) Formation of regions shall be permitted in Scotland and Wales, replacing the population of Greater London with that of the most populous city in each nation.

(h) Every region shall have a unicameral parliament to make its own regulations within United Kingdom and national law, and raise any taxes that are inadequately funded from the national parliament. Part-time participation in regional parliaments is to be encouraged.

Article 6 allows creation of regional governments. The objective is to put the citizen at the centre of joined-up government and therefore Integrated Care Boards should be included in the structure.

7.

(a) Each nation shall operate efficient, fair, and humane policing, justice, and detention systems.

(b) Save for regional governments, each nation is responsible for all its affairs and laws that are neither reserved to the United Kingdom government nor defined in this Constitution.

(c) The United Kingdom government shall have a coordinating role wherever this makes economic and practical sense, without usurping the sovereignty of the nations. It shall provide United Kingdom-wide services with the consent of the nations.

(d) The United Kingdom government is responsible for international obligations that require uniform application, including supervising financial, aviation, shipping, and international rail services. Any nation may take its own responsibility for international trade obligations that do not require internal borders, excepting these services, if approved by vote of its people.

OVERSEAS TERRITORIES OF THE UNITED KINGDOM

8. All territories taking the defence guarantee or relying on the United Kingdom for foreign representation shall abide by the minimum United Kingdom standards and those international agreements other than for trade (which are optional), that would apply to them if they were a nation of the United Kingdom. They shall be represented in the People's Council and the United Kingdom parliament. Representation for those with populations less than 30,000 may be on a shared rotating basis. In all other respects, they are at liberty to follow their own constitutional arrangements, approved only by their citizens. Their citizens are not United Kingdom citizens. The United Kingdom parliament may agree exceptions to minimum standards where they relate to economic matters that should be adjusted for differences in living standards. Constitutions of each Overseas Territory must allow for citizens to choose integration with the nations of England, Scotland, Wales, and Northern Ireland, and to leave the United Kingdom completely, at their own democratic determination.

Article 8 treats all overseas territories equally apart from their size. The constitutional distinctions between fragments of empire (both inhabited and uninhabited), the sovereign bases in Cyprus, and the Crown dependencies are redundant.

CITIZENS

9. A person is the citizen of their nation of birth, naturalisation, or parentage, and save for citizens of the Overseas Territories has unrestricted rights throughout the United Kingdom. All citizens of the United Kingdom can stand for election and vote

in United Kingdom elections and in their nation of residence (or, if non-resident, their nation of citizenship). For local and regional elections, a residence requirement is a matter of national sovereignty. National United Kingdom citizenship can be changed without fee apart from usual passport issuance fees. Passports shall state: "Citizen of the United Kingdom of Great Britain and Northern Ireland – *nation*." A person may only hold one United Kingdom citizenship; in the case of minors with two parents holding different United Kingdom citizenships, the parents shall choose.

Article 9 makes every UK citizen, a citizen of one of the nations. A person can only have one citizenship but can change it voluntarily, for example if his/her parents were of different British nationalities. Voting in UK and national elections is open to all citizens without a residence requirement, ending the second-class treatment of some British nationals born outside the UK who have never lived permanently in the UK.

10. All citizens of the nations forming the United Kingdom have the following rights:

   (a) to reside anywhere in the United Kingdom;

   (b) to good administration;

   (c) to access to documents at only the direct cost of printing, postage, packaging, and handling;

   (d) to petition the local authority and parliament(s) of residence and nationality, and the United Kingdom parliament, and to have such petition heard fairly and without prejudice;

   (e) to take complaints of unfair, unreasonable, or incorrect treatment by any government to an ombudsperson;

   (f) to stand for election to any legislature of residence or nationality and to the People's Council;

(g) to take complaints of any general legislative failing or abuse by government to the People's Council and to take requests for constitutional change to the People's Council;

(h) to life, freedom, and security;

(i) to respect for private and family life and the right to marry any person irrespective of gender;

(j) to freedom of expression and freedom of speech (the latter subject only to constraints regarding defamation, security, media impartiality, and evidence requirements);

(k) to freedom of thought, conscience, religion, association, and assembly, including the right to demonstrate;

(l) to a fair trial in civil and criminal matters and to jury trial in criminal matters, each juror having the right to use matters of conscience and/or conviction as the basis for voting;

(m) to property and peaceful enjoyment of possessions;

(n) to prompt issue of a passport;

(o) to receive official communications in English, Welsh, Scots Gaelic, Irish Gaelic, or Ulster Scots according to their residence and preference;

(p) to privacy in their personal and business communications, save for matters of the utmost national security;

(q) to have any adverse regulatory finding and/or court judgement arising from error, third-party fraud, or false allegations, expunged from the record, and to receive fair and prompt compensation for loss from any appropriate State authority. The compensation right also applies to businesses and organisations where a claim arises from State error;

(r) to receive prompt and fair compensation for any error or failure by the State to provide a monopoly state service;

(s) to form or join a political party to advance any viewpoint and contest legislative elections;

(t) to have their welfare, safety, security, good health, and quality of life prioritised over commercial interests, including fair pay that ensures an existence worthy of human dignity;

(u) to lead lives free of bullying, harassment, and expropriation of assets or income.

Article 10 sets out all rights of citizens, including to a passport (currently at the Home Secretary's discretion). There is a new right to compensation for certain errors. The State should act as a protector against erroneous judgements arising from error or fraud (State error only for businesses and organisations). Article 10 (u) will strengthen protections against serious errors such as the Post Office Horizon scandal.

11. The following are prohibited:

    (a) the death penalty;

    (b) torture or inhumane or degrading treatment or punishment;

    (c) slavery and forced labour;

    (d) arbitrary, indefinite (save for whole-life sentences for the most heinous crimes), indeterminate, and unlawful detention; and also arbitrary rulings without justification;

    (e) discrimination in the enjoyment of the rights and freedoms secured by this Constitution;

    (f) deportation of citizens unless the citizen has freely consented to deportation and evidence has been tested in a British court;

(g) denial of entry (including denial to a citizen lacking a current passport and denial to a person having residence rights in the United Kingdom);

(h) the collective deportation of foreigners;

(i) deportation of asylum seekers and refugees to any state which is not clearly committed to equivalent rights to those in this Constitution;

(j) detention of any woman in the third trimester of pregnancy and for three months thereafter;

(k) cancellation of a passport (save at the citizen's request in case of loss or change of name), refusal to issue a passport, and deprivation of citizenship, unless evidence has been presented that the citizen holds a current passport of another nation;

(l) refusal of either parole or early release in the case of a prisoner who declines to admit guilt.

Article 11 is a list of prohibitions, intended to remove any doubt about the State observing international conventions. Citizens gain the right to refuse deportation. Britain should not dump its responsibilities onto other nations by refusing entry to its citizens, nor should it engage in mass deportations and similar abhorrent practices. Pregnant women gain the right not to be imprisoned in their third trimester or immediately after giving birth. Any remaining sentences of indefinite imprisonment for public protection are void.

12. Persons who marry a United Kingdom national are entitled to naturalisation after both five years' residence and three years' concurrent marriage on satisfaction of a basic language test in English, Welsh, Scots Gaelic, Irish Gaelic, or Ulster Scots according to residence. Children reaching age 18 who have lived permanently in the United Kingdom for at least five years must

be given automatic naturalisation. All other naturalisations are a matter for the nations.

13. Lawful residents have all the above rights except for the right to vote in United Kingdom elections and referenda and to stand for the United Kingdom parliament. Except where given in this Constitution, naturalisation rights are a matter for the sovereign nations. Lawful residents have the further right to family reunion. They may be deported only for serious criminal offences, to a state where their rights will be respected.

Article 13 defines the rights of lawful residents. It allows family reunion and restricts deportation of lawful residents to serious criminal offences.

14. In all legal, criminal, administrative, and commercial matters, for both the State and all organisations and citizens, automated aids to making decisions may only be used where they have been independently audited for accuracy of judgment using test cases compared to human decisions and where accuracy has been independently established to be fewer than:

    (a) one error in five hundred cases for employment decisions;

    (b) one error in five thousand for other administrative decisions including State decisions, other than those regarding employment and any legal uses;

    (c) one error in ten thousand for legal decisions excluding criminal prosecutions;

    (d) one error in one million for legal decisions involving criminal prosecutions.

    This standard applies to governments, including elections, and all organisations and individuals in their dealings with others. Citizen appeals against State misuse are to an ombudsperson;

citizen appeals against commercial misuse are to an independent tribunal.

Article 14 limits reliance on the judgment of systems, including (but not limited to) AI, unless audited for accuracy. The State and all businesses using systems-based decisions must meet this accuracy standard before relying on AI or automated systems.

THE STATE AND THE CITIZEN

15. The State must:

    (a) treat citizens, permanent residents, and refugees with dignity, respect, equality, and good faith;

    (b) protect children and young people while encouraging their development;

    (c) provide coordinated support and assistance to those in need;

    (d) observe the seven principles of public life, namely Selflessness, Integrity, Objectivity, Accountability, Openness, Honesty, and Leadership. In any situation where there is an overriding need for confidentiality, openness may be deferred but only for a reasonable period of time, by stating that the matter is confidential but will be disclosed as soon as possible.

16. Regional or national governments (where there are no regions) shall provide free education until at least the age of eighteen. They shall provide a high standard of technical education for all adults. Parents have primary responsibility for teaching children the difference between right and wrong; schools should teach civic responsibility, critical thinking, and creative subjects, but limit teaching violent history except in the context of the perils of aggrandisement, imperialism, and hatred.

17. No law shall restrict the freedom of:

    (a) academic institutions in their research and teaching;

    (b) the media in all formats, subject to accuracy of facts, evidence for opinions, correction of errors, avoidance of character assassination, and not suppressing the public interest in facts;

    (c) artistic and cultural expression.

Article 17 defines academic, cultural and media freedom, and imposes accuracy responsibilities on the media.

18. Citizens may follow any lawful occupation that enables their chosen standard of living.

19. Employers and employees may form associations to protect their rights provided that:

    (a) such associations do not create barriers to entering any trade, profession or occupation;

    (b) disputes are resolved through negotiation or mediation;

    (c) strikes and lock-outs are permitted only in relation to employment terms. They must not be used to avoid conciliation;

    (d) only the military, security and police services are denied the right to strike.

Article 19 allows formation of unions and employers' organisations and requires conciliation. Strikes and lockouts are allowed in relation to employment terms only.

20. Rights and redress:

    (a) The rights of citizens set out in this Constitution and, where appropriate, the rights of permanent residents and refugees, are fundamental and must be observed by the State at all times. No bureaucratic process may avoid or limit them in any way.

(b) Every national government shall appoint a minister for redress, who shall ensure that ombudsperson and inquiry rulings and compensation promises shall be dealt with swiftly, fairly to the citizen or permanent resident, and accurately. Regional and local governments shall make analogous provision for matters within their remit.

The final sentence of Article 20 (a) prevents backsliding by the State. See also Article 37.

THE LAW

21. Courts, tribunals, inquests, prosecutions, and administrative proceedings (collectively referred to as "courts"):

    (a) The nations must provide independent courts and tribunals, an independent judiciary, an independent appeal capability, and independent inquests. The United Kingdom parliament provides the Supreme Court. No parliament may interfere with the judicial system save for correction of failures of independence of the judiciary.

    (b) Any offence against United Kingdom law must be tried in the nation of residence or, for non-resident citizens, the nation of citizenship. For other non-residents any convenient court may try the matter.

    (c) All parties to a case must be allowed to state their argument.

    (d) The courts must ensure equal and fair treatment and hear cases within a reasonable time such that neither witness memory is impaired, nor relevance ceases.

    (e) Any court may order that free legal advice and assistance be given to a defendant in a criminal, family or administrative case, unless it is clear to the Court that the defence has no prospect of success. Costs of any legal aid are to be borne by the nations, which may regulate the fees charged by lawyers.

(f) A court may also order free legal representation in court in its absolute discretion.

(g) Secret and *ad hoc* courts are prohibited.

(h) Criminal and administrative matters may be appealed within the nation and then to the Supreme Court, unless the first level of appeal in a nation rules that a case is hopeless.

(i) Hearings may only be in private in matters of the utmost national security. Judgments shall always be in public but may be anonymous to protect minors and the security services.

(j) The use of civil penalties and administrative proceedings is only allowed where there is an unrestricted right of appeal to a court. The appeal may lie through an independent tribunal in the first instance.

(k) Civil proceedings must be held in the nation of residence of one of the parties. If the parties are unable to agree or both parties are non-resident, then a court in any jurisdiction may determine the matter.

(l) Digital records archived with version history have equal validity with paper documents.

(m) Litigation funding for both civil and criminal cases is permitted and may not be restricted.

(n) All judgements given in courts of higher status than magistrate or equivalent, and all findings of inquests, shall be published.

(o) Rulings on United Kingdom law are binding throughout the United Kingdom.

FIRST-DRAFT CONSTITUTION OF THE UNITED KINGDOM

Article 21 requires independent courts, prohibits secret courts, provides some legal aid, and prohibits penalties without a right of appeal to a court. The habit of picking the pocket of citizens without due process is banned. Digital records become admissible.

22. Liberty and penalties, including commercial penalties:

    (a) No person may be deprived of liberty except by a court or by pre-trial detention where a serious criminal offence is alleged. In the latter case, a court must approve the detention within 48 hours and then re-approve it at least every two months. No such detention may exceed six months, nor may it be renewed. A new detention is permitted only if it arises from a new and unrelated charge.

    (b) A person cannot be deported unless a court approves the deportation and can only be held in administrative detention prior to a hearing on an application to the Court.

    (c) No person or organisation other than a court or tribunal with appeal rights may impose penalties or sanctions. Contracts with prices varying by payment terms are permitted provided no payment term amounts to an unfair penalty. Contract renewal prices may not exceed those charged to new customers.

    (d) Every person accused of a criminal offence has the right to avoid self-incrimination and is presumed innocent until a court finds otherwise.

    (e) Criminal charges must be brought promptly and explained to the alleged offender, who must be given the opportunity to prepare a defence.

    (f) Private prosecutions are only allowed in magistrates courts or equivalents. All other prosecutions are a matter for the Crown prosecution service, which must consider the widest public interest before proceeding.

(g) A charge of fraud, theft, embezzlement, or false accounting that relies on data processed through a computer system may only be prosecuted if an independent systems expert has certified that the system was secure, free of all errors that might be relevant to the prosecution, and could not be compromised nor data amended by any other person during the period relating to the alleged offence.

(h) Expert witnesses may only give evidence if they have no connection whatsoever, through any familial, employment, or contractual relationship, with any party in a case.

(i) Where two or more persons wish to appeal separate convictions that appear to have a common element, a single appeal shall be heard on behalf of all those whose names have been disclosed to the Court. If further affected persons subsequently come to light, the Appeal Court shall examine their connection to the original appeal and certify whether they fall within its scope, in which case their convictions will also be overturned by the certificate given by the Court.

(j) Courts must provide interpreters where needed in criminal cases.

(k) Use of any form of surveillance is subject to review by the High Court or equivalent.

(l) The State may levy penalties and impose sanctions provided there is a right of appeal to an independent tribunal and thence a court at no cost or delay to the person penalised or sanctioned.

(m) No person or organisation may receive a bonus, award, or incentive for collecting any penalty or enforcing any judgement.

Article 22 establishes the right to liberty. Article 22 paragraphs (f), (g), and (h) are a further protection against systems' abuse by the powerful, arising directly out of recent scandals. This Article also prevents private levying of fines, a practice that has grown extensively, and limits sanctions that have no right of appeal.

23. Other legal provisions:

    (a) Non-disclosure agreements may only be used to protect matters of commercial confidentiality by businesses and citizens. All State uses are prohibited except for official secrets that have the potential to be useful to an enemy.

    (b) An injunction naming specific persons or organisations can only take effect when they are aware of it.

    (c) An injunction that does not name specific persons or organisations can only take effect when individuals and organisations that may be affected have been informed of its terms and given a reasonable opportunity to comply with them.

    (d) No part of the State shall use the threat or fact of legal costs to prevent citizens from holding the State to account and, accordingly, no legal costs exceeding one-tenth of average annual wages or salaries may be recovered from any person or group of persons taking action against any part of the State.

    (e) Inheritances may be taxed but not confiscated and accordingly, *bona vacantia* is abolished.

    (f) Any law that has been modified twenty times in total shall be repealed and re-enacted before further modification. For this purpose, every amended sub-paragraph in every paragraph shall count as a separate amendment.

(g) Any law that is more than fifty years since its original enaction shall expire on its fifty-fifth anniversary unless re-enacted.

Article 23 paragraphs (a) to (e) prevent the State from abusing citizen's rights. Article 23 paragraphs (f) and (g) ensure that the law can be easily understood and is up to date and relevant.

24. All parliaments and the People's Council shall provide for hybrid work capability, and used or tested regularly, so that emergencies can be handled effectively and members who are unwell, pregnant, or in a caring role, or who have a disability are able to participate.

25. The public have the right to observe all parliamentary proceedings in person, subject to safety, security, and capacity limits. Parliaments must allow for at least fifty public observers for every one hundred members or part thereof.

26. Lobbying:

    (a) Elected representatives may not promote the interests of any person or organisation for reward, and must disclose any memberships, employment, contracts, or interests that may affect their judgement.

    (b) Ministers and advisers serving in any government must disclose all contact with lobbyists immediately. They shall give fair and equal access to any community group or organisation.

    (c) Civil servants and members of the People's Council are debarred from all lobbying activities.

SOCIAL OBJECTIVES

27. Primary responsibility for social objectives rests with the nations. The United Kingdom government may set minimum standards and provide technical and quality support to the nations. Regions acquiring economic powers are also responsible for social objectives, but may rely on their nations or other neighbouring regions for any appropriate part of them.

28. Social objectives include: good healthcare, education for the modern world, resilient transport, dignified employment, good-quality housing, effective and dignified social care, provision for old age, disability, and child support.

RELATIONS BETWEEN THE ARMS OF GOVERNMENT, FINANCIAL EQUALISATION, AND LEGAL RELATIONS

29. Elected governments:

    (a) All governments are chosen by the people and must cooperate with each other for the benefit of the people.

    (b) They are accountable to their elected parliaments or authorities, which have the right to investigate any aspect of their work.

    (c) Subject to equalisation of financial resources, the arm of government providing a service shall raise the required revenue by taxation and be free to define the scope and details of its service, with approval by the people. User fees may only reflect the direct cost of providing a service plus a fair allocation of overheads incurred in providing that service, and may only be charged for an efficient, accurate, and prompt service. Waiting for a service shall not be extended by any form of reclassification. Excessive user fees and double charging under different headings are prohibited.

Article 29 imposes a duty on governments to cooperate. Combined with the clear responsibilities in the constitution, this should end turf wars and blocking moves.

30. Arms-length bodies, statutory bodies, state-owned companies, regulators, committees and all other units of the British State howsoever constituted:

    (a) All non-elected bodies (even if they have non-executive directors) are accountable to the elected parliament or body most closely approximating to their geographical responsibilities, and which elected body shall supervise them.

    (b) Supervisory responsibilities include appointment and termination of directors, quality of services provided to the public, and investigation of complaints to search for common causes.

31. Where responsibilities are divided or overlap, any differences must be settled by negotiation. If this is not possible, the matter must be put to those people affected by vote. The outcome must be approved by all affected legislatures and published.

Article 31 requires governments to settle disputes by negotiation or send the matter to a vote.

32.

    (a) Equalisation of financial resources shall be achieved by annual financial transfers in either direction between:

      (i) the United Kingdom government and the nations;

(ii) each nation and any regions formed within it;

(iii) where there are no regions, each nation and each first-tier local authority within it;

(iv) where regions exist, each region and each first-tier local authority within it;

(v) each first-tier local authority that is not unitary and each second-tier authority within it.

(b) The transfers shall be calculated annually based on average population and economic output of the appropriate unit of government.

(c) The calculation shall ensure that for the first twenty years after this Constitution comes into force, no government or local authority area has a per capita standard of living below 98.5% of the average standard of living for the entire United Kingdom.

(d) The data and calculations shall be provided by National Statistics each year.

(e) Where an Integrated Care Board spans more than one region or multiple Integrated Care Boards form one single region, financial equalisation shall also apply, with an adjustment set by National Statistics for demographic variations.

(f) The federal parliament has the right to review national taxation and benefit policies to ensure that the equalisation rules are not being malignly manipulated, but if a constitutional amendment is needed, shall refer the matter to the People's Council.

(g) The extent to which equalisation benefits individual households is a matter for the sovereign nations.

33. Nations, regions, local authorities, and Integrated Care Boards may enter into agreements with each other for matters within their competence, such as to share resources for the benefit of the people.

34. In the event of any conflict of law or service to the people in any joint arrangements, the highest standard of service shall be adopted. If any dispute continues, the matter shall be put to the relevant people, i.e., those affected in any way, by vote.

35. Each nation and region make their own laws consistent with this Constitution and United Kingdom law, approved by the relevant people.

36. Minor boundary adjustments between nations, regions, local authorities, and Integrated Care Boards are allowed where they simplify provision of public services. Any boundary change affecting more than 5% of the population of any area involved in the change, shall be approved by the relevant people. Any national proposal to leave the United Kingdom, or local proposal to change nation, shall require at least 50% of the total electorate proposing to change, to vote in favour.

37. Governments have only the powers granted in accordance with this Constitution. No law, regulation, or administrative action may negate, curtail or restrict this Constitution.

Article 37 limits government power. This is necessary because the Establishment is used to doing as it wishes.

38. Civil contingency and disaster planning are primarily the responsibility of the nations. All governments shall report triennially to the people on the state of such planning and explain all assumptions made.

FOREIGN AFFAIRS

39. Foreign affairs are the responsibility of the United Kingdom parliament, answerable to all the people:

    (a) Significant proposed international agreements or changes that are significant shall be approved by the people in two stages, the first to authorise negotiations and determine their scope, and the second to approve the final text, where possible on a line-by-line basis.

    (b) All trade agreements and amendments, without exception, must be subject to this two-stage approval.

    (c) The objectives of foreign policy shall be to promote a harmonious world without hatred or aggrandisement, in which humankind does not do long-term damage for short-term advantage; to improve the education, skills, health, and living standards of poorer countries; and to promote international order and respect for international law.

    (d) The United Kingdom shall not resile from any international body or agreement in order to adopt lower standards.

    (e) All foreign affairs shall be conducted in cooperation with national and regional governments.

Article 39 makes the UK government responsible for foreign affairs. It requires trade agreements and other significant agreements to be approved in principle before negotiation, and again in detail. This would prevent a situation such as Brexit, when a majority believed Britain would at least stay in the single market (i.e. all remainers plus some leavers), only to get a more extreme policy forced upon them by a small group of politicians. It would also prevent unnecessary concessions being made in negotiating trade agreements.

40. National and regional parliaments may ask for consent of the United Kingdom parliament (not to be unreasonably withheld) to negotiate specific international agreements that are necessary for them alone. If granted consent, the resulting agreement must be approved by the United Kingdom parliament, in addition to gaining the People's Assent of the nation or region, and must not conflict with any existing laws or agreements. Such agreements may extend to trade-related matters if they do not cause any internal border in the United Kingdom and are made by a nation or by several nations acting together.

Article 40 makes clear that national and regional governments may negotiate international agreements necessary only for themselves, rather than pass the matter up to the UK government. Only national parliaments can ask for and negotiate limited trade agreements.

MILITARY, SECURITY, POLICE, AND EMERGENCY SERVICES

41. The armed services, external borders, and security/intelligence services are the responsibility of the United Kingdom parliament. The police and emergency services are the responsibility of the nations. Regional parliaments have the right to manage their police and emergency services, if approved by the people. The police must be operationally independent of all parts of the State and enforce laws equally.

42. Only the United Kingdom parliament has the authority to permit offensive military action. It may do so only to prevent an armed attack upon the border integrity of the United Kingdom, or at the request of a foreign government or international agency seeking

assistance, or in extreme cases of threats to significant British interests.

43. Civil defence is the responsibility of the nations, in cooperation with the United Kingdom parliament. Emergency aid may be provided by the armed forces on request by a national or regional parliament.

44. Persons who suffer ill-health, and the families of those who lose their life, in any military, security, police, or emergency services, shall be fully supported by the relevant government.

CULTURE, EDUCATION, AND RELIGION

45. Culture, the Arts, and education are the responsibility of the nations and regions. National parliaments shall ensure financial and academic independence of universities. The United Kingdom parliament may support and encourage centres of excellence in research for the benefit of all nations. The United Kingdom parliament shall be responsible for promoting British values abroad.

46. Regions within a nation shall coordinate school curricula with the national government and each other. National parliaments shall ensure ample provision of further education of a high standard, covering all appropriate technical, vocational, and non-vocational subjects.

47. Statistical, weather, and mapping services are the responsibility of the United Kingdom parliament. Music and sport are the responsibility of national or regional parliaments.

48. Religious observance is a private matter beyond the remit of the State. The people are not obliged to follow any religion, even if established. No official or state ceremony may include a mandatory religious element.

Article 48 needs debate. The UK is increasingly agnostic, yet church and State are intertwined. Perhaps it is time for the two to separate? The demise of the House of Lords will remove power from the bishops (although they could stand for the People's Council). Should a coronation, for example, be religious?

49. Issuance of Charters is the responsibility of the United Kingdom parliament, which shall also review existing Charters and terminate those that are obsolete.

INFRASTRUCTURE AND ESSENTIAL SERVICES

50. Infrastructure planning is reserved to the nations, which shall coordinate their plans with the United Kingdom parliament. City planning and housing planning are matters for the regions (where they exist) in conjunction with first-tier local authorities, and otherwise jointly for the nation and first-tier local authorities. All other planning is a matter for first- and second-tier local authorities to agree between themselves. The United Kingdom parliament shall specify minimum standards for building and infrastructure.

Article 50 distinguishes infrastructure, city, housing, and local planning, but leaves minimum standards with the UK parliament.

51. Housing, water, drainage, power and energy supplies, transport, education, healthcare, supply of nutritious food, and many internet facilities, are essential infrastructure services. If these are supplied by monopoly or duopoly providers as defined in Article 52 (b) *et seq.*, then they must at least be regulated to include:

   (a) supply at a fair price without profiteering;

   (b) prohibition of borrowing in any currency other than sterling, and prohibition of borrowing in sterling at interest rates more than 1% above the rate at which a similar business can borrow from a major United Kingdom bank or on the open fixed-interest market;

   (c) restriction of use of derivatives to genuine hedging of variable supply costs;

   (d) requirements to continue capital investment for the benefit of future generations;

   (e) restriction of dividend payments to a fair return on capital, including new investment;

   (f) prohibition of measures that, in the circumstances prevailing at the time, evade responsibility for completion of any service, procedure or other benefit to the public.

Article 51 protects essential services from the financial abuses that have caused so much poverty and caused damage to the environment. Rent extraction should end. Financial abuses such as offering compensation that cannot be utilised are also prohibited by Article 51 (f).

52. Prevention of businesses exploiting the citizen:

   (a) The scope of this Article applies to water and drainage, transport, power, debt collection, logistics and distribution, all local monopoly services such as (but not limited to) student accommodation, public housing and car parking, and any critical supplies that are reasonably necessary for life. It also applies to all businesses, even if controlled from outside the United Kingdom, if they have factors that make them unique or factors that make them an effective monopoly or duopoly in the United Kingdom.

(b) There shall be a presumption that a business that satisfies either of the following tests within the geographic area it supplies is an effective monopoly or duopoly:

  (i) Fifty percent or more of households have an account with the business or have used the services of the business within the past two years.

  (ii) Forty percent of adults have an account with the business or have used the services of the business within the past two years.

(c) Businesses that fall within this Article and are privately owned, even if their ownership is outside the United Kingdom, shall offer their services to all persons without discrimination or restriction and shall not discriminate between or unfairly select or dismiss their suppliers, save for variable external costs of supply. Their contracts must be compatible with United Kingdom law, enforceable in the United Kingdom courts, and no foreign court or tribunal shall have effect.

(d) Businesses that artificially divide their customer accounts or service provision into multiple units shall be treated as one for the purposes of this Article and Article 50.

(e) The United Kingdom parliament shall regulate all businesses falling within this Article to ensure fair treatment of all suppliers and customers and to ensure that persons (whether as customer or supplier) and taxpayers are not exploited or bullied.

(f) National and regional parliaments (the regions acting together where necessary) may take into public ownership monopoly/duopoly utilities and businesses with similar characteristics that provide essential services, at least 90% of the activities of which, by population served, are within their borders. Such ownership shall be on a not-for-profit basis in which the interests of all stakeholders are balanced, and long-term investment is maintained. Compensation paid to the previous owners shall be the lowest of:

(i) any previous price the utility or business was sold for, if it was publicly owned at any time within the previous 100 years, ignoring changes in the value of money and business changes by the utility while privately owned, and after deduction of any increase in debt;

(ii) the market value of the utility on the day before its proposed nationalisation was announced;

(iii) the market value of the utility on the day legislation to nationalise it was granted by the People's Assent;

(iv) the net asset value of the business reduced by any losses made through any form of direct or indirect financial engineering while privately owned, and specifically any dividends paid to owners in excess of the lower of 1% of turnover or 3% of equity capital, and any interest paid to owners exceeding 3% of principal, and also reduced for any other type of financial engineering that benefited current or previous private owners without incurring losses;

but loans repayable to independent third parties who have no connection directly or indirectly with the present or any previous owners, shall be honoured. An independent accountant's certificate is mandatory for this exception to apply.

Article 52 brings all tech businesses that are essential to daily life within the same rules as utilities, including businesses that are local selective monopolies such as car parking and student housing, thereby restricting monopoly behaviour in most cases identified by Professor Christophers[41]. It requires fair treatment of all people whether as customers or suppliers and provides power to regulate new forms of financial engineering, grants nationalisation powers to the nations and (with limits) the regions, but severely restricts the price that may be paid. Tech companies now provide essential infrastructure, and their services are to be provided fairly in accordance with UK law. In nationalisations, genuine third-party debt shall be honoured, but debt acquired as part of a financial engineering scheme is to be wiped out. This protects third-party lenders, while forcing those who have extracted rents from the British public to give something back. The difficult situation of present owners not being those who undertook financial engineering (as may be the case at some water companies) is passed to the present owners, who will have to consider whether they have grounds for action against previous owners. If they bought a dud, that is their mistake. It is possible that this Article could pass some losses to pension funds, but somebody has to pay.

53. In the case of monopoly and duopoly utilities operating in more than one nation, these powers are also available to the United Kingdom parliament in consultation with national parliaments, or to national parliaments acting together.

GOVERNMENT ACCOUNTS, THE NATIONAL DEBT, AND TAXATION

54. Every unit of government from the United Kingdom government to the lowest tier of local authority shall produce annual accounts to the standard of Generally Accepted Accounting Practice. All such accounts shall be drawn up as at 31 March each year, audited, and published by 30 September. Accounting at 5 April is abolished.

55. National borrowing is the responsibility of the United Kingdom parliament. Interest costs of debt existing when this Constitution comes into force shall be apportioned to the nations by gross domestic product at the same date. New borrowing can be on the authority of the United Kingdom parliament, national or regional parliaments and the authority requiring such new borrowing shall reimburse all interest costs arising and issuance costs, from its taxation revenue. Accounts shall allocate new borrowing according to who pays the interest cost. United Kingdom debt issued within this Article, and debt previously issued as a charge on the consolidated fund of the United Kingdom, is a charge on all nations of the United Kingdom.

Article 55 splits existing debt costs by GDP. New borrowing is distinguished as a service by the UK parliament to national or regional parliaments that bear their own costs. If there is a desire for national governments to build their own credit record, this Article will need amendment.

56. Only the United Kingdom parliament may levy a value added tax, customs and excise duties, consumption, and withholding taxes. That parliament may not levy any other taxes unless expressly approved by all parliaments. The United Kingdom parliament may not levy taxes on the incomes of individuals, nor on the profits of businesses, nor on capital gains. Taxes on wealth are a matter for

the sovereign nations. Where regions exist, the division or levels of income, capital gains, and corporation taxes are to be negotiated by the respective parliaments and approved by the people. All other taxing powers, including taxes not previously levied in the United Kingdom, rest with the nations and regions.

57. Financial engineering:

    (a) Financial arrangements that benefit any individual or organisation at the expense of society are presumed contrary to the public interest and therefore void unless it can be shown that there is a genuine net benefit to society.

    (b) Interest may only be deductible against tax if the relevant loan was directly used, within six months of availability of the loan, for capital investment.

    (c) Derivative assets and liabilities should be shown in accounts with an accountant's report certifying that the counterparties and any further counterparties of offsetting derivatives are in all ways independent of ownership and associated parties. If this is not given, such assets and liabilities must be reported as "Other assets/liabilities (as appropriate) that may be connected to the company's owners".

    (d) Public-sector contract charges for special services and requirements to maintain facilities that are a basis for remunerating private-sector service providers must be clear, fair, and not unreasonable. No action may be taken against any public service to enforce terms that breach this rule, existing contracts included.

Article 57 (b) ensures that taxation advantages are only given for genuine capital investment and not for financial engineering or rent-extraction purposes. 57 (c) will expose some other methods of extracting money from the public. 57 (d) deals with contracts for public services that contain excessive and sometimes hidden remuneration requirements. Many examples can be found. See 'Our lives in their portfolios'[41].

HEALTHCARE

58. Healthcare, including essential dental care, is primarily the responsibility of the nations and regions. Healthcare is to be free at the point of use, except for non-residents where they do not benefit from reciprocal agreements. Healthcare is either to be funded by the regions or, where there are no regions, the nations, or by insurance. In the latter case, underwriting for medical conditions and by age are both prohibited; insurance premiums may only relate to per capita costs by lowest tier of government in a recent period; insurers shall be backstopped by the nation; the nations shall agree the scope of insurance cover so that nobody is denied treatment or illness prevention measures; and insurance premiums shall be shown as "Insurance - Healthcare" on tax demands.

Article 58 sets out responsibilities for healthcare, which is to be free at the point of use. Insurance is allowed as an alternative to taxation, but the nations must act as re-insurers. Age and medical underwriting are banned.

59. The United Kingdom parliament retains overall responsibility for care quality and standards, laboratories, medicine approval, and health protection. The United Kingdom parliament shall determine any exceptions from universal healthcare.

BUSINESS, THE ECONOMY, COMMON REGULATION, AND STANDARDS

60. The United Kingdom parliament shall regulate matters benefiting from common standards, such as (but not limited to) all forms of transport, the environment, natural resources, energy, water, drainage, power supply, weights and measures, telecommunications, postal services, the media, and gambling. Such measures may be regulated by national parliaments if that is the present case or transferred to national parliaments either by the United Kingdom parliament, or by request of the people of a nation in accordance with this Constitution.

Article 60 is a more general common standards clause, omitting drug and alcohol abuse. The omission allows liberal nations to experiment with rehabilitation schemes, whereas other nations may prefer criminal sanctions. Nations have the right to resile from other common standards.

61. In regard to criminal matters, common standards including sentencing apply to charges that would be heard in a crown court or equivalent and higher courts, but not to matters that would be ordinarily dealt with by magistrates or equivalent.

62. Any authorisation for professional or regulated services granted by a nation or by a private sector professional body shall be valid throughout the United Kingdom.

63. Regulation of companies and provision of a public register is a matter for the United Kingdom parliament. Defunct entries shall be removed after 25 years.

Article 63 deals with the register of companies and corrects an omission in current law that prevents some obsolete entries in the companies register from removal.

64. This Article applies to all organisations whether state or private, outsourced functions and services, and to multiple organisations that have the effect of subverting its intent:

    (a) The total annual remuneration of the highest-paid person in any organisation shall not exceed fifty times the total annual remuneration of the lowest-paid person, calculated on a full-time equivalent basis by contracted hours.

    (b) Organisations may only provide a single source of remuneration (other than pensions) to their directors and employees, but their pay may be variable according to results. Directors who are company owners may also receive dividends. Benefits in kind are allowed so long as they are available to all directors and employees of an organisation and the total value at market prices of any person's benefits shall not exceed ten percent of the highest-paid person's remuneration, excluding pensions.

Articles 64 to 66 are intended to prevent corporate abuses and limit inequality.

65. There shall be no cartels, abusive pricing or other methods of limiting competition. All regulation of businesses shall include a simplified method for starting new small businesses.

66. Consumer pricing must be fair and open. The nations must provide simple, effective and economical grievance procedures for consumer complaints about any business.

67. Monetary policy is the responsibility of the United Kingdom Central Bank, answerable to the United Kingdom parliament. The bank has power to issue notes and coins. Any profits made by the bank belong to the people and shall be paid to the United Kingdom government, which shall equally reimburse losses. Appointments

to the bank's board and decision-making bodies must be approved by the United Kingdom parliament.

Article 67 reserves monetary policy to the UK parliament, delegated to the UK Central Bank. The name 'Bank of England' is implicitly discontinued, since the Bank serves all the nations. The question of central bank independence should be revisited in the light of possible recent monetary policy mistakes.

68. Commercial banks in Scotland and Northern Ireland retain power to issue banknotes provided they are fully underwritten by the United Kingdom Central Bank. Commercial banks in Wales may be given this power if the people of Wales request it and the bank(s) have their head offices and at least 50% of their customer accounts located in Wales.

69. Subject to this Constitution, the nations shall determine their own policies in relation to agriculture, forestry, fishing, land use, the environment, and the sea bed.

70. The United Kingdom parliament shall determine export permissions for armaments and weapons of war.

71. The nations shall determine reserve stocks and rotation arrangements for contingency reserves enabling adequate food, water, power, and medical supplies in adverse conditions, and for emergency rationing.

72. The nations and regions shall ensure adequate supply of modern fuel-efficient homes that are affordable by everyone. "Right to buy" is permitted at a discount of not more than 5% to market prices, where this does not restrict a nation or region from achieving adequate supply.

Article 72 imposes a duty to ensure supply of modern affordable and fuel-efficient homes, leaving it to the nations and regions to choose between private and public building.

73. The United Kingdom parliament shall legislate to ensure that tenants are protected from abuse, and rented properties are properly maintained. Tenants who honour their obligations must be given at least twelve months' notice to leave, but may give three months' notice to the landlord if they wish to leave. Continuous or repeated rolling notices are prohibited. Landlords may only select tenants on the basis of evidence that they can pay their rent.

Article 73 protects tenants from abuse, including inadequate maintenance, and limits the ability of landlords to throw tenants out at short notice.

PENSIONS AND BENEFITS

74. The state pension system is the responsibility of the United Kingdom parliament. The parliament shall consider the merits of changing slowly from a pay-as-you-go system to a funded pension system. Pension costs are to be met by the nations, and pensions may be supplemented by the nations.

75. National parliaments shall determine minimum benefit levels, so that no person shall be hungry, cold, or without a home. Benefit costs are to be met by the nations.

ELECTIONS TO PARLIAMENTS AND LOCAL AUTHORITIES

76. The term of elected bodies and their rights:

    (a) The United Kingdom parliament shall be dissolved five years after first meeting.

    (b) Each national parliament shall cease to have effect four years after first meeting.

    (c) Each regional government shall be supervised by a parliament serving identical terms to its nation.

    (d) Local authorities that are unitary shall cease to have effect four years after first meeting.

    (e) All other local authorities shall cease to have effect three years after first meeting.

    (f) Every parliament and local authority shall meet by the seventh working day after declaration of the results of the election.

    (g) United Kingdom and national parliaments acquire all the rights, rules, and privileges of the House of Commons, which they may modify within this Constitution. Regional parliaments are not successors to the House of Commons and write their own rules within this Constitution.

    (h) Only the People's Council may require or authorise an early election.

    (i) Otherwise, existing law shall apply to the calling of elections and to by-elections. If the matter is not clear, existing parliamentary law shall apply.

(j) The loyalty of elected members of national and regional parliaments is to their people; that of the United Kingdom parliament is to all the people.

(k) Parliamentary rules shall encourage debate and consensus.

(l) Physical and virtual markings of separation are prohibited.

(m) All votes shall be secret.

(n) A government or local authority that loses an election shall resign by the day on which its parliament or governing body first meets following that election. It may continue on a caretaker basis if there is no clear choice of a new government or governing body on the part of the electorate.

(o) Overlapping elected terms are abolished.

(p) Elected members of the United Kingdom and national parliaments may style themselves MPUK, MPEN, MSP, MS and MLA.

Article 76 gives parliaments (but not regions or local authorities) all the rights and privileges of the present House of Commons which is implicitly abolished. It sets their terms as five, four or three years according to seniority, and gives the power to call early elections to the People's Council. Article 76 (j) is intended to ensure that all elected persons can sit in the UK parliament and the new parliaments, by voiding the Parliamentary Oaths Act. Secret votes are required so that elected members may put their constituents first when there is a conflict with parliamentary party management. Secret votes also reduce the potential for performative legislation which has no benefit for the people.

77. Elections, manifestos and referenda:

(a) Electoral registration, election authorities and returning officers adopt existing law, with the exceptions noted in this

Article. However, secure online voting and uniquely coded ballot papers distributed by post are permissible alternatives.

(b) Referenda are optional for national and local matters at the discretion of national parliaments, save for boundary matters.

(c) Where voting takes place in person, identity may be evidenced by the poll card plus a signed declaration that the voter is the person named on the card.

(d) The electoral system for the United Kingdom parliament shall give fair representation to all collective points of view held by more than 5% of the electorate in each nation separately. The minimum age for voting in the nations, for elections and referenda specified in this Constitution, excluding those authorised by a national parliament, shall be 16. The nations and Overseas Territories shall be represented in the same numbers as in the professional group of the People's Council (Article 99). The electoral systems and rules for national and regional parliaments shall be determined by the sovereign nations.

(e) Political parties are not obliged to publish manifestos. If they choose to do so and wish their manifesto to be binding if elected, they must list all their policies separately. Ballot papers must allow electors to say "Agreed" or "Refused" against each separate policy, or alternatively approve all policies of the elector's chosen party.

(f) Manifestos must clearly state the objectives of policies. Words that do not clearly state proposed changes such as (but not limited to) "review", "modernise", "reform", "balance", and similar, are not allowed. Specific policy choices must be clear and not misleading.

(g) A manifesto commitment will be binding and presumed to have the People's Assent if all the following are true:

  (i) the candidate is elected;

  (ii) a majority of the votes cast (not necessarily those voting for the elected candidate) agree the policy;

  (iii) the party sponsoring the candidate has published a statement of intent detailing the proposed legislation at least one month before polling day;

  (iv) only minor technical corrections to those proposals are made in the parliament;

  and therefore voters may choose a candidate according to the voting system for the election, and separately choose policies that may be promoted by different candidates or simply refuse certain policies of their chosen candidate, but contradictory choices will both be invalid.

(h) Multiple referenda for different levels of government may be conducted at the same time, but not at the same time as elections for legislatures or elections to the People's Council.

(i) For every intended referendum, the appropriate parliament shall debate the issues and vote for or against the referendum, and a summary of its debate and vote shall be prepared by the clerks.

(j) For every intended referendum, the appropriate government or other unit of the State shall prepare a concise statement of its view with a reasoned recommendation to the people.

(k) For every intended referendum, campaigning groups may prepare short statements for or against the referendum.

Campaigning groups may be political parties or *ad hoc* committees formed for one particular referendum.

(l) All these views shall be published as an official communication to every voter in a booklet of typically fifteen to thirty pages per referendum issue, at least one month before the vote. Different levels of government shall coordinate referendum dates in advance. The appropriate government shall publish the timetable for items (h), (i), (j), and (k) in good time. Not more than four referenda for any one level of government may be held on the same date.

(m) Election communications are governed by the general rules in Article 90, which apply at all times.

(n) No referendum question may be reopened for ten years after a previous similar one.

(o) Each nation shall appoint an electoral registration officer for non-resident citizens who have never lived in the United Kingdom.

Article 77 is the basis of election and referendum law. It permits alternatives such as secure online voting and barcoded ballot papers and abolishes requirements for identity evidence for in-person voting. The requirements for manifestos to be sufficient to grant the people's assent are set out. Rules for the conduct of referenda so that voters are properly informed are here, and a referendum question may not be reopened for ten years. Article 2 (d) overrides this for the Belfast agreement, which has different provisions. Note also that a nation choosing not to allow national, regional or local referenda would still participate in UK referenda, in any called by the People's Council to establish the people's assent, even for national legislation, and in boundary referenda.

78. Every elector shall be given an annual voucher to donate to a political party. Vouchers shall be valid for fifteen months from date of issue. The value of the vouchers shall be set by the United Kingdom parliament annually. All other donations in cash or kind, fund raising, payments in kind, and club membership fees designed to raise political funds are prohibited. The costs of vouchers shall be a United Kingdom expense; electoral administration costs shall be borne by national governments.

LEGISLATION

79. Each and every parliament is sovereign in its sphere of responsibility as defined in this Constitution. It can make, alter and repeal law provided that:

    (a) in any bicameral parliament both chambers must agree the proposed law, and neither may override the other;

    (b) the People's Assent is given to each law, and accordingly, Royal Assent is abolished;

    (c) secret laws and secret decrees are prohibited;

    (d) no law shall give any executive or official power to alter the law;

    (e) no law shall deem or assert something to be the case when it would not otherwise be so;

    (f) no law shall restrict the ability of the judiciary to review any aspect of such law;

    (g) only laws made in accordance with articles 114 to 119 may amend or override this Constitution in any way;

(h) memoranda of understanding are prohibited. They are replaced by primary law or secondary regulations approved by vote in the relevant parliament and by the People's Council.

Article 79 re-establishes parliaments as in control of governments, rather than the present system whereby governments use parliaments to impose their will on the people. It prohibits ouster and deeming clauses: these are autocratic practices that should never have seen the light of day.

80. Legislative procedure:

    (a) In forming law, each legislature shall provide adequate time to properly scrutinise all proposed legislation.

    (b) Secondary regulations shall only take effect after debate and vote in the legislature, and approval by the People's Council. The "negative process" is abolished.

    (c) All draft legislation and legislation introduced to any parliament shall set out the evidence supporting any policy or, if there is no such evidence, include a prominent statement that there is no evidence to support the proposed policy. Evidence suggesting that the policy may be incorrect or capable of a better solution must also be published.

    (d) If draft or introduced legislation is to amend any prior laws, the effect of such amendment (if passed) must also be published.

    (e) Guidance for implementation of any legislation may only be explanatory. It cannot usurp the functions of the legislatures or the People's Council.

Article 80 requires legislatures to debate and vote on all regulations, whereas currently parliament has little say in them. Policies must be based on evidence, or the lack of evidence admitted. Publishing the effect of amendments to prior laws will avoid the indecipherable nature of some legislation, thereby reducing the scope for error.

81. Local authorities, whether unitary or two-tier, must consult their electorates on all proposed by-laws. They may either publicise the proposed by-law widely and seek comments, or (if allowed by their nation) call a referendum to approve the draft by-law. If they choose the first course of action and their nation permits referenda, a demand for a referendum may be submitted by one-tenth of their electorate within three calendar months after the closing date for comments. No by-law may come into effect until at least four months after the closing date for comments unless approved in a referendum. One-tenth of the people, in a nation that permits referenda, may also submit a proposed referendum to a local authority, which shall arrange the referendum within six months.

OMBUDSPERSONS

82. Every parliament and local authority shall appoint an independent ombudsperson to investigate complaints of unfair, unreasonable or incorrect treatment of individuals or families by government departments and State agencies:

    (a) The public can take a complaint to the most convenient ombudsperson (for example, of residence).

    (b) If necessary, that ombudsperson can refer the matter to another ombudsperson.

    (c) Ombudspersons have unlimited powers of investigation and immunity from legal action.

    (d) Any ombudsperson can recommend a change in general rules or a specific exception, and the government or agency concerned must accept the recommendation.

(e) Local authorities can either participate in a regional or national ombudsperson service, or collectively share an ombudsperson.

(f) All costs arising must be reimbursed by the department or agency that is the subject of complaint.

(g) Ombudspersons shall arrange remote hearings where necessary.

(h) Any ombudsperson can also refer a matter to the People's Council for further consideration.

(i) Ombudspersons must have professional qualifications as defined for the professional group of the People's Council, or be former members of the People's Council.

(j) Existing ombudsperson services shall, where practicable, be merged with this service.

Article 82 creates an ombudsperson service for all governments. Elected representatives should not be spending a large part of their time and support resources on fixing bureaucratic messes. In time, this should, for example, reduce the trials and tribulations reported by someone who had escaped the labyrinthine benefit system[97].

THE PEOPLE'S COUNCIL

83. The People's Council is entirely the voice of the people. Former politicians and peers may stand for election to the professional group if qualified and otherwise to the general group. All members must forgo political activity including membership of political parties during their service and cannot serve until three years have elapsed since leaving active politics. This period may be reduced by a year if they have worked for two years full-time in a charity for people who experience homelessness, poverty, dispossession,

or are asylum seekers or refugees. The People's Council makes its own decisions as to what subjects to investigate and how to approach any matter, based on communications from the public and this Constitution.

Articles 83 to 110 are about the People's Council. *This mainly elected representative body will replace the Privy Council and the House of Lords, but instead of being legislative and political it will be apolitical to ensure that the people's voice is heard.*

Article 83 requires its members to forego political activity while serving and ensures its complete independence by allowing it to control its own work.

Article 84 defines its formal responsibilities. Articles 85 to 97 then set out the detail of how it will meet its responsibilities. Articles 98 to 111 say how it will be elected and remunerated, including a provision for sortition (Article 107). There will be two groups of elected members, one for regulated professions and the other for everyone else. Electors who are members of regulated professions can only stand and vote in that group; all other electors stand and vote in the general group. The purpose of this is to ensure that some professional skills are present among the membership while allowing anyone to stand for membership. Each group will have a two-part election, for leadership positions and all other members, and every elector will have three votes, one for leaders and two for all other members, within either the professional or general group.

The heart of this constitution is to ensure that the people's voice is heard, ending the attitude that government can get on with ruling as it likes.

84. The responsibilities of the People's Council:

   (a) It will be responsible for ensuring the independence of British institutions, so that they cannot be manipulated by ephemeral political fashions.

(b) It will enforce high standards in the State and carry out investigations, including arms-length bodies.

(c) It will act as a clearing house for referendum and constitutional change requests.

(d) It will provide a channel to ensure that the public voice is heard.

(e) It will act as the final arbiter on all legislation and international agreements (see Article 93).

(f) It will supervise the work of all ombudspersons, to ensure that they are serving the public to protect against arbitrary or unfair behaviour by any part of the State.

(g) It will supervise a facts hub, to be funded by the United Kingdom government and maintained by National Statistics, providing a straightforward summary of facts about the economy, trade and all public services for the nations.

(h) It can refer matters to the Constitutional Court (Article 119).

85. Every agency, department, committee, organisation, regulator, arms-length body, and institution playing any part in the British State, together with every media organisation by whomsoever owned, but excepting the military, emergency, police, and secret services, shall declare to the People's Council whether it is independent of government and of all political parties, or none. The People's Council shall audit such independence and publish its assessment. An audited organisation may make changes and request a reassessment once, before the original assessment is published, but must complete changes within six months of the original assessment. Audits should be repeated every twenty years, and earlier if there is public disquiet. Every body exercising judicial powers or having the right to impose penalties or restrictions of

private rights, and every body having any influence over the electoral system, must be independent and have an effective independent appeal procedure.

86. The factors to be taken into account in establishing independence shall include, as a minimum:

    (a) who appoints directors or senior officers: governments must have no influence, even indirectly;

    (b) how the organisation is funded: governments must have no control or influence over the level of funding, even if they provide resources from taxation;

    (c) whether there are any familial, friendly or commercial relationships between any members of any government, any other non-independent organisation, and senior members of the subject organisation;

    (d) whether any government has any legal or licensing rights over the organisation;

    (e) whether the organisation earns more than one-third of its revenue from government contracts, counting all governments as one entity;

    (f) whether it has made or received any political donation in the last five years;

    (g) whether it is accountable to any parliament.

    (h) Statutory regulators and bodies whose objectives are set by any parliament or law can never be classed as independent.

87. The People's Council may receive public complaints about poor, unethical, corrupt, or disreputable conduct, and also conduct that breaches any part of this Constitution, by ministers, officials, and any part of the State including public-sector services (even

when outsourced). It has power to investigate any government, authority, state agency, regulator, committee, department, and media organisation. It shall publish reports. In extreme cases it may suspend persons from ministerial appointments, subject to a right of appeal to the High Court or equivalent. It may also refer cases to other bodies where appropriate (including advisers on ethics and ministerial behaviour) for consideration, and will refer any suspicion of criminal matters to the police for priority investigation. It must document all investigations; any person investigated shall have a right of representation. If a matter requires skills that the People's Council lacks, it may seek expert advice.

Article 87 provides an overriding power so that advisers cannot be neutered by politicians.

88. The People's Council may receive public complaints about disreputable media behaviour, including (but not limited to) biased analysis and opinion, false equivalence of extremist views with common sense, and character assassination. It has power to investigate media and publish reports; it may require publication of corrections, subject to a right of appeal to the High Court or equivalent. It may also refer suspected breaches of this Constitution to the courts (see Article 119).

89. Investigations:

    (a) The People's Council may investigate any government, department, agency, regulator, arms-length body and committee, and also any private-sector body that is a monopoly or duopoly provider of an essential service irrespective of ultimate ownership (housing, food, electricity, water, fuel, transport, education, healthcare, visas, telecommunications, and all internet-based services included) to ensure that the best standard of service and redress is provided and rents or excess profits are not extracted via any form of financial engineering. Its enquiries may extend beyond the United Kingdom, and it may make use of technical experts to assist its enquiries.

(b) The People's Council may review any rule book operated or referenced by any department of government, agency, arms-length body, committee or regulator for any purpose. It may recommend changes in the interests of fair treatment of the people and, if the recommendations are not adopted without good reason, may refer the matter to the appropriate parliament.

90. Official and political communications and all media communications:

(a) At all times, every communication that is official, political (including all media opinions, interviews and reports), or may have any influence no matter how remote in how any person votes, shall be clear, fair, and not misleading. All such communications in every type of media shall be approved by a senior person who shall keep records of approvals for release on request to the People's Council.

(b) Government, political and media corrections of errors, whether under Article 88 or any regulatory or standards requirement, shall be given urgently and with equal prominence to the original error. This includes visibility, duration, and placement. Corrections of advertising or political communications that are not clear, not fair, or are found to be misleading, must be sent or displayed to the same targets that received or saw or heard the original communication. If this is not possible, they must be broadcast or published to a wider audience. The United Kingdom parliament shall determine penalties for non-compliance. The courts may strike down any election or referendum result that may have been influenced by non-compliant communications or foreign agents and require a new election or referendum.

91. Calling referenda (applicable to internal matters in the nations only when a national parliament has adopted referenda), other than changes to this Constitution:

    (a) Ten percent of any electorate, or five percent on a proposal by the People's Council, supporting a demand for a referendum at United Kingdom, national or regional level (in those nations allowing national and regional referenda) may require a referendum to amend the law on any matter save for constitutional changes.

    (b) Proposed legislation shall be included in rough draft form.

    (c) The People's Council may amend the proposed referendum wording for clarity. It may defer a request for up to five years on grounds of triviality or extremism and, on resubmission, require twenty percent of the relevant electorate to support the request.

    (d) If the referendum achieves a majority of those voting and at least 40% of the electorate vote, the appropriate government shall comply within the same time period as in Article 96.

    (e) A proposal for a referendum cannot give rise to any criminal offence, even if the subject or mere mentioning of it is a criminal offence.

Article 91 (e) is intended to permit challenges to matters that governments have restricted.

92. The People's Council shall provide a public access service for general issues about British governance, politics, and the State. It

may treat common comments as indicating a specific point that should be referred to a parliament for consideration, or it may conclude that a people's referendum is needed to change the law. In the latter case, Article 91 applies.

93. How the People's Assent may be given to a law passed by any parliament or to an international agreement:

   (a) When a majority of those voting agreed with a policy in an election, and a statement of intent and objectives that is clear, fair, and not misleading, was published in good time, then the People's Council shall certify to the appropriate parliament whether, in its view, any changes from the original proposal are only minor technical corrections and accordingly the People's Assent is given.

   (b) In the case of significant international agreements and all trade agreements at United Kingdom level, the people must approve proposed negotiation terms in an election manifesto or referendum prior to commencement of any negotiations.

   (c) In all other cases that do not fall within (a) above, and always for international agreements and proposals for honours, the People's Council shall consider whether the proposed law as approved by a parliament or international agreement as negotiated, or proposed honour, clearly agrees with public opinion and, if it has any doubt or considers that the law or honour is controversial or unwanted or the agreement may be defective, then the People's Council shall choose one of these three courses of action by debate and vote:

   (i) to decide itself whether to agree or reject the legislation, honour or international agreement by further vote; or

(ii) to convene a group of at least 50 (for local and regional matters), 100 (for national matters) or 200 (for United Kingdom matters) citizens chosen randomly to debate and vote secretly on the issue; or

(iii) to refer the legislation or international agreement to a compulsory referendum, even in a nation that has not adopted referenda for national/local matters; and these three choices are in the absolute discretion of the People's Council.

(d) All members of the People's Council shall participate in United Kingdom assent. Only those members representing a nation, may participate in national and regional assent.

(e) All votes by the People's Council, under this and other articles, are secret.

94. The People's Council may also convene a group of at least 50 (for regional matters), 100 (for national matters) or 200 (for United Kingdom matters) citizens, chosen randomly, to debate and vote secretly on any issue prior to preparation of legislation by any parliament. This may be requested by the relevant parliament or initiated by the People's Council.

95. The People's Council has the rights to initiate legal action in the name of the people, to summon witnesses and to enter any premises, interview any person and inspect any documents and computer records and systems (the latter even if held outside the United Kingdom if pertaining to anything in the United Kingdom), on seven calendar days' notice. Current operational matters in the military, security, and police services are excluded but may be investigated retrospectively, with protection of sources.

96. Approval of referendum requests:

(a) All requests for referenda to change the law, and all requests for constitutional amendments, must be addressed to the People's Council. The People's Council may amend wording for clarity, in conjunction with the requesters, and such amendments shall not invalidate the request. If the number of supporters meets the threshold (and in the case of constitutional amendments, the timetable) then the People's Council shall have six months to consider the request. On approval, it shall direct the appropriate government to arrange the referendum or constitutional change vote:

   (i) within a further six months for local authorities;

   (ii) within a further one year for national governments; and

   (iii) within two further years for United Kingdom wide matters; and

   (iv) in accordance with this Constitution for constitutional changes;

   but (i) and (ii) only apply in a nation that has not adopted referenda, in respect of boundary change requests.

(b) The People's Council may deny approval, by vote, for any reason.

97. All non-confidential work of the People's Council shall be published, including summaries of all debates, discussions and investigations. The People's Council and its members shall have immunity from legal action. Crown immunity is abolished.

MEMBERSHIP OF THE PEOPLE'S COUNCIL

98. Membership of the People's Council is open to all citizens and permanent residents over the age of twenty-one on the day an election is held, who are neither in any elected position nor employed at a senior level by any government, parliament, institution or media organisation within the scope of Article 85. There shall be two elected groups of members and a further sortition group, but all members shall have equal votes. The elected groups are:

   (a) members of regulated professions, as recorded by the United Kingdom government (including non-resident citizens who would be regulated if practising the same profession in the United Kingdom) and who will usually be full-time members;

   (b) general members, including some part-time members. Prospective general members shall state whether they wish to be part-time or full-time at the election.

99. At creation, the number of members for regulated professions shall be in the national representations: Northern Ireland eight, Wales thirteen, Scotland twenty-one, England thirty-four. Those Overseas Territories with populations exceeding 30,000 shall be allocated one place each and other Overseas Territories one place to rotate among them. The professions shall operate a pooled candidate list. A person who is qualified for this group may not stand or vote for the general group and shall inform the electoral registration officer of this fact. These elected members in the professional group serve a four-year term renewable once, but may stand down for a period between their terms of membership. Acquiring or giving up membership of a regulated profession takes effect for this purpose at the next election.

100. All other persons are represented by and can stand for the general group, the members of which shall be selected at creation in national elections in the representations: Northern Ireland twenty-one, Wales thirty-four, Scotland fifty-five, England eighty-nine. Those Overseas Territories with populations below 30,000 shall be allocated two places to rotate between them and other Overseas Territories one place each. These elected members serve a three-year term renewable twice, but may stand down for a period between any of their terms of membership. After three years, the membership of the general group shall increase to the representations Northern Ireland thirty-four, Wales fifty-five, Scotland eighty-nine, England one hundred and forty-four.

101. Elections to the People's Council:

   (a) Elections for the two groups of the People's Council shall be at different times of the year approximately six months apart. All elections for one group shall be on the same day. The first election shall be for the professional group.

   (b) Regulated professions shall choose one professional body to act as election secretariat and coordinate candidate nomination and election arrangements. The United Kingdom parliament shall reimburse reasonable costs of the secretariat.

   (c) National governments shall arrange elections for their nations in the general group and meet the costs.

   (d) They shall advertise widely and may conduct webinars to provide interested persons with information.

   (e) Prospective candidates may submit a resumé and statement of why they wish to serve on the People's Council to the professional group secretariat or national government, as appropriate, to be published to electors. Such documentation may include references to material published in any format and any evidence of standing in their community or their occupation.

(f) The nations and Overseas Territories shall coordinate their election arrangements.

(g) Campaigning for election is limited to addressing groups of electors in person or via webinars, in both cases with ample facilities for questions.

(h) Nominations open three months before polling day, and close one month before the said date.

(i) Every elector has one vote for the leadership group and two votes for the general group, within either the regulated or general membership.

102. Within each of the two groups of membership, there shall be two lists of candidates. The leadership list in the professional group has eleven members: one, two, three and five respectively for the four nations, and the leadership list in the general group has eighteen members: two, three, five and eight respectively for the four nations. The main lists are reduced in number by the number of elected leaders; if there are insufficient leadership candidates, then the main list acquires corresponding extra members. Candidates for the leadership list may also stand for the main list and be elected there if not chosen by the leadership ballot.

103. Persons who are members of political parties must resign their membership within fourteen days of election, for the duration of their membership and neither participate in political activities nor rejoin a party until twelve months after ceasing to be a member of the People's Council.

104. The operating costs of the People's Council shall be met by the United Kingdom parliament on behalf of all the nations.

105. Members shall be compensated for reasonable expenses including travelling second class, accommodation in three-star hotels and essential home-office equipment (if not provided through other employment) and shall be remunerated as follows:

   (a) The employers of members who are in employment shall be compensated for normal pay and direct overheads and shall allow full- or part-time absence as necessary.

   (b) For self-employed members in partnerships, equivalent compensation shall be paid to the partnership.

   (c) For self-employed members who are not in partnership and also for members in limited companies where they are the only employee, the member shall be compensated directly for lost or potentially lost income and, in the case of companies, the company shall be compensated for overheads. All such compensation shall be based on previous accounts.

   (d) For members who were retired, resigned from their previous occupations, or not in work prior to election, an honorarium shall be paid equivalent to 125% of the previous year's United Kingdom average income for employment, pro-rata for hours worked.

   (e) Part-time members may be rewarded for non-conflicting work provided their total reward on a full-time basis does not exceed the amount they would be rewarded if working full-time for the People's Council.

106. The leadership list for each election is intended to allow citizens to choose direction of the People's Council and to allow civil society leaders to stand for election. If a vacancy occurs after election,

the People's Council has authority but not obligation, to co-opt a member from the main list of either group to the vacant leadership position. The initial leadership (formed from both groups in combination) shall decide how to phase in responsibilities, provided the People's Assent can be considered when needed by legislatures.

107. Sortition to ensure complete representation of society:

(a) In addition to the two elected membership groups, there shall be additional members serving a single term of three years on a full-time or part-time basis, chosen by the national governments by lot. Any chosen person working for an employer must be released on the same terms as for other members, but may object on grounds that his employment cannot easily be replaced. Any chosen person having caring responsibilities must be fully supported in those responsibilities. Any chosen person completely unable to serve, for example because of chronic illness or disability, and in some cases of employment and self-employment, shall have the option of serving at a later date (in which case the additional member place is cancelled meanwhile) or proposing a substitute (within the same demographics) of their choice.

(b) The additional members form part of the general group and the number of them who agree to serve in accordance with (a) shall be subtracted from the number elected in the general group for each nation.

(c) National parliaments shall determine whether to include additional members chosen by lot, based on the demographics of candidates for the general group by age, gender, and income, promptly after nominations close for the general group. The maximum number of additional members shall not exceed three, five, eight, thirteen for the four nations. Overseas Territories are excluded from additional members. Every national government shall maintain demographic data for the whole nation that enables additional members to be chosen promptly.

(d) Additional members participate in teams with other members in all votes and areas of responsibility of the People's Council. They are to be provided with appropriate mentoring.

(e) A person who has served as an additional member may subsequently stand for election for two further three-year terms in the general group, or, if qualified, for one further four-year term in the regulated group.

108. The People's Council shall maintain an administrative secretariat in a place that is neither the seat of the United Kingdom government, nor the seat of any national government. For matters requiring debate and discussion affecting the whole of the United Kingdom, it shall meet in various locations in any of the nations that are accessible from the whole of Great Britain and Northern Ireland. For matters requiring debate and discussion at a national level, the national members shall meet in various locations within their nations. Meetings are open to the public, except when there may be a serious confidentiality requirement. A summary of non-confidential discussions and decisions taken shall be published by the secretariat within three working days. Visual and audio recordings may be published on the same basis.

109. Allocation of tasks:

(a) Allocation of tasks for part-time members shall be appropriate for their circumstances, and provisions shall be made for members who have disabilities or caring responsibilities.

Members working from home shall have a second person, with relevant experience, to refer to for assistance and guidance.

(b) Allocation of tasks for all members shall include participating in teams of three, including at least one member from the professional group. More complex tasks may require five members, with at least two from the professional group, or seven members with at least three from the professional group. Part-time members and especially those normally working from home shall have the opportunity to participate in investigations. In all other cases, members shall be allocated tasks that they are interested in, qualified for, or able to perform under the guidance of an appropriate member. Task allocation may be revised at the discretion of the leadership.

110. Members may style themselves "PC" after their names. The form of address "Right Honourable" is abolished. Previous members of the Privy Council may not use this style or form of address.

111. Members of the People's Council must exhibit the highest standard of personal, ethical, and moral behaviour. Members shall suspend activity if subject to professional or criminal investigation and must resign if not cleared within six months of suspension. Members must not have any conflict of interest; the applicable standards shall be the highest of those of all regulated professions.

HONOURS

112. In general, awarding honours for political services is abolished:

(a) There shall be no spoils of office.

(b) Existing holders of honours awarded for political services may not display medals in public, nor may they use or cause to be used any special style of address. Peers of the realm who were ennobled for political services (including hereditary peers whose forebears were ennobled for political services) may no longer style themselves in such a way nor exercise any rights arising from their ennoblement.

(c) The use of all titles, including "Sir", is prohibited.

Articles 112 and 113 deal with the honours system, which is in severe disrepute.

113. The People's Council may approve a request by ten percent of the local, regional, national or the entire electorate for an honour, excluding a peerage or knighthood, to be awarded for service to the appropriate public, under Article 93 (c) above.

ENTRY INTO FORCE

114. This Constitution shall come into force on 1 January in the fourth year following approval by the people in a referendum. Electors may vote for or against the entire Constitution or on a line-by-line, sentence-by-sentence, paragraph-by-paragraph, or article-by-article basis (provided the intent of the proposed change is clear), in which case particular clauses and sub-clauses may be removed. The procedures for preliminary referenda by the nations and for drafting the Constitution shall be determined under previous law. The Constitution will be approved if 50% of the total electorate and a majority of nations excluding the Overseas Territories approve it. Any individual term voted separately by any elector will be excluded if the votes approving it (including those voting in favour of the entire Constitution) are fewer than the

number of those excluding it (including those voting against the entire Constitution). If the effect of this rule is to cause a serious inconsistency, it shall be put to a further referendum within three months.

115. The existing United Kingdom parliament shall invite proposals for a city to be the seat of the new United Kingdom parliament (and therefore the seat of the United Kingdom government), by passing suitable legislation within six months of the referendum approving this Constitution and implementing a further referendum to approve the choice within a further six months. It shall allow alternative cities in England, Scotland and Wales to compete and their proposals to be included in the vote (see Article 5). If no legislation is passed or no proposals received or no referendum held, Manchester shall be selected.

Article 115 deals with the seat of the UK government. It is impractical to place the seat of government in Northern Ireland because of the high travel costs and environmental damage that would arise. The default provision is intended to thwart blocking moves in the present House of Commons.

CHANGES TO THIS CONSTITUTION

116. Excepting the final sentence of Article 114, this Constitution may only be amended once in every fifteen years, to take effect from 1 January fifteen years after its entry into force and every subsequent fifteenth anniversary:

    (a) Only the people may propose changes. No criminal offence may arise by proposing a change.

    (b) By the first working day of January three years before the potential amendment date, but not more than six months earlier, the People's Council shall invite draft amendments and state the closing date.

(c) Proposed amendments shall be submitted to the People's Council within nine months of such invitation, or at such later date as specified as the closing date, with supporting signatures by ten percent of the electorate.

(d) The People's Council shall take legal advice to ensure that the proposed amendments are clear, fair, and not misleading; and that they do not cause internal conflicts within the Constitution, and if necessary shall adjust the wording in consultation with the promoters.

(e) It is permissible for two proposed changes that would have opposite effects to be put to the people provided the contradiction is clearly explained and defined.

(f) The People's Council shall cause an explanatory document to be prepared that sets out what the effect of the proposed changes may be, including any improvements or reductions in citizen's rights and improvements or reductions in trade that can reasonably be expected, and identify any changes that appear to be nebulous or difficult to evaluate. Those promoting each proposed change may submit a statement of why the change is recommended. All parliaments shall debate the proposed changes and vote on them. A summary of their debates and the votes recorded shall be included in the explanatory document. Every government at regional, national and United Kingdom levels has the right, but not the obligation, to include a short statement of their viewpoint for each proposed change that relates to their level of government. In the event that regions wish to comment on a national or United Kingdom matter, they should, so far as is practical, make a joint statement. The resulting document must be sent in print to every elector. Two or more electors living at the same address may, if they wish, indicate that they only need a single copy.

(g) A referendum to approve the proposed changes shall be held within twenty-four months of invitation of draft amendments.

(h) Each amendment shall be voted on separately, but in the case of contradictory amendments, approval of both proposed changes shall invalidate both.

(i) An amendment will be approved if 50% of the total electorate and a majority of nations excluding the Overseas Territories approve it.

FURTHER TRANSITIONAL PROVISIONS

117. Transitional arrangements:

(a) Any existing law that conflicts with this Constitution becomes null and void on the date this Constitution enters into force.

(b) All international agreements that conflict with this Constitution must be renegotiated to eliminate such conflicts within three years. If, at the expiry of three years, such renegotiation has not been successful, then notice to terminate such agreements must be given within three months, the notice period to be in accordance with each agreement.

(c) All existing trade agreements shall be reviewed by the People's Council within ten years of this Constitution coming into effect and the People's Assent confirmed. If such assent is denied, the agreement must be renegotiated within three years of denial or terminated in accordance with its provisions.

(d) Ongoing costs that apply before and after this Constitution enters into force shall be divided appropriately between governments.

(e) Article 20 (b) applies to ongoing compensation claims.

118. Development of the United Kingdom, nations and regions:

(a) Elections for the United Kingdom parliament shall be held within six months of this Constitution entering into force.

(b) Elections for national parliaments shall be held within one year of this Constitution entering into force.

(c) Detailed proposals for regional governments in England may be brought forward two years after this constitution enters into force.

(d) Proposals for regional governments in Scotland and Wales may be brought forward seven years after this constitution enters into force.

(e) Overseas Territories, all being sovereign, shall, within five years of this Constitution entering into force, either legislate to conform to this Constitution or cease taking the defence guarantee, foreign representation, and legal appeals, in which case they lose all rights under this Constitution.

(f) In any interregnum between election dates under previous law and under this Constitution, existing parliaments may continue subject to previous law. However, if an election is due under previous law within six months before the deadline for new elections under this Constitution, then the life of the previous parliament may be extended by not more than six months.

THE CONSTITUTIONAL COURT

119. The High Court or equivalent shall act as a first-tier Constitutional Court, with direct appeal to the Supreme Court. The People's Council has the right to refer any suspected breach of this Constitution to the Court, and the Court may impose such remedies as are appropriate. Any citizen, group of citizens, or organisation wishing to take a matter to the Court shall first ask the People's Council to consider it and report to them. They may proceed with an application to the Court provided they include the report of the People's Council in their submission.

APPENDIX A: THE PRIVATE FINANCE INITIATIVE (PFI)

It is worth spending a few minutes understanding why this policy failed. **I researched it in 2002, and most of the paragraphs that follow are taken from private presentations delivered that autumn. They have stood the test of time.** I offer this as one detailed example of state failure. My original sources are no longer all available, but I have added some recent footnotes. In 2023, the debt overhang caused by both large political parties adopting PFI is still with us.

The basic concept of PFI was that public capital expenditure plus ongoing operating costs would be replaced by the purchase of a complete service package including the capital construction cost. Roads and prisons were special cases, the first because of the high cost of construction compared to ongoing maintenance, the second because it was thought that private security guards could break the stranglehold of the Prison Officers Association, at least in prisons for lower-risk offenders.

The concept took off after the 1997 election, spreading rapidly into hospital and school construction. In both of these, the basic concept of buying an entire service package had to be modified: clinical care and teaching were to remain the province of the State, with just building maintenance and support services, such as catering, bought in as a service package.

The question that needs to be addressed is this: is the service fee payable to the contractor appropriate for the deflationary financial environment we are moving into? Does it fairly reflect lower interest rates and reduced returns on capital? Obviously, if it is too generous then we will all pay dearly as deflation spreads. The signs from the contractors are ominous. The building industry seems to be delighted with PFI, which may be because its costs of tendering are reimbursed. Most major projects are operated by a specially created company. If the project is financially successful, the profits can be extracted. If it goes wrong, the special venture company can be liquidated with no impact on the parent.

Now, obtaining facts about PFI is remarkably difficult. The terms of the service contracts are generally commercially confidential. There is much political noise about the capital being spent, particularly on hospitals and schools, but no information about the ongoing cost of that capital. A little has been unearthed by academics and think tanks, notably Leeds University, the King's Fund, and the Office of Health Economics (OHE, an independent research body). The two major sources of information, though, are government itself, and the public sector unions, both of which must be discounted as vested interests peddling their wares. Go to almost any government department website and you will find a completely uncritical adulation of the concept of PFI. Visit any public sector union website, and you will find broad assertions about neglect of the public interest, for which read workers' interest. Neither is helpful.

One surprise as I researched this subject was that there is more information about PFI projects in Scotland than in England and Wales. One side effect of devolution is that the Treasury's iron grip

APPENDIX A: THE PRIVATE FINANCE INITIATIVE (PFI)

is a little looser in Scotland. Thus some of the examples for which figures are available come from Scotland. Even so, the true costs are still usually 'commercially confidential'. The following staff figures (full time equivalents) are available for the new Edinburgh Royal Infirmary (Table 6)

	1996	*Projected*	*Change*
Medical	544	499	-8.2%
Nursing	2,144	1,844	-14.0%
Clinical support	899	866	-1.4%
Administration	802	556	-30.6%
Ancillary	502	312	-38.0%

Table 6 – Effect of proposed private finance initiative at Edinburgh Royal Infirmary (2002)

The average number of times an NHS bed is occupied in a year has stabilised at fifty-four. But one estimate that I have seen is that Edinburgh Royal Infirmary will need to put eighty-eight patients per annum through each of its beds; nobody knows how this is to be achieved. The problem is in the costs:

Capital cost of new hospital	£210m
Annual service fee	Commercially confidential[98]

As a general principle, it seems that annual servicing costs are to be met by reductions in beds, reductions in headcount, and sale of city centre sites as hospitals relocate to greenfield out-of-town sites. There have been suggestions that other economies would be imposed on non-PFI hospitals to pay for the servicing costs of PFI hospitals, but these are impossible to substantiate.

In Kidderminster, threatened closure of the local hospital led to election of an independent MP. The closure arose directly from the introduction of a new PFI-financed hospital in Worcester[99]. In

APPENDIX A: THE PRIVATE FINANCE INITIATIVE (PFI)

Norwich, there has been a noisy campaign against relocating to an out-of-city site, reported in the *British Medical Journal*[100]. It seems that the costs to the community, of extra travel compared to travelling to city centre hospitals, do not count. Meanwhile in Durham, a dispute over the services to be provided by the contractor led to a doctor calling an ambulance at night to move a patient between two buildings[101]. Design errors mean that the pharmacy is located next to the mortuary but without a waiting area, so patients and relatives queuing at the pharmacy see the mortuary admissions; the ambulance bay is too small and is blocked if four ambulances arrive together; cold water taps run hot, depriving parts of the hospital of fresh drinking water. Design errors have also been reported at the new Cumberland Royal Infirmary in Carlisle. Both Durham and Carlisle have experienced bed reductions and increases in waiting lists[102].

I managed to locate these figures for Durham hospital in a report in *The Guardian*[101]:

Capital costs

Construction cost	£67m
Financing cost (capitalised)	£18m - a one off payment for interest costs

Annual costs

Contractor's basic fee	£7m pa
Ancillary services	£5m pa

Trust resources

Annual funds for capital costs	£5m (including non-PFI outlying hospitals)

Table 7 – PFI costs at Durham hospital (2002)

As you can see, the contractor is taking £12m a year for thirty years to build and operate a building costing £67m. There will be a forced shrinkage in this trust's services of up to £5m annually in order to balance the budget. Once again, deflation can involve activity shrinkage as an alternative to price reductions. Over the thirty-year contract the total cost of this PFI will be £360m, for a building costing just £67m.

According to the OHE, PFI projects are compared with conventional exchequer finance using a discount rate of 6%[103]. The discount rate is the annual reduction of future values to translate into today's values. This discount rate is deliberately high, because it is intended to capture the transfer of risk to the private sector. Most of the risk with large-scale building projects is timetable slippage. The terms appear to be that the revenue earning period is reduced by the extent of any delay in commissioning a hospital. It also appears from the OHE and other studies that a capital sum is allowed for risk in the bidding process, so contractors may be being paid twice over. What is certain is that paying an annual fee for thirty years when risks are mainly in the first two years, breaches the basic principle that reward should be matched with risk. It follows that there is intense pressure on contractors to cut corners in design, as Durham and Carlisle have discovered, and contractors are then able to refinance their operations at lower costs and pocket the windfall.

There is another problem with that 6% discount rate. The OHE says that it should be 4% to allow for properly pricing risk once only, while the Institute for Public Policy Research prefers 5%. In my view, both are too high, because neither figure allows for a deflationary future. The structure of PFI itself is likely to reinforce that deflation. Absent any inflation, and even a discount rate of 4% is more than the historical rate of interest, which has fluctuated between 2% and 3% in real terms for centuries. The higher the discount rate, the more attractive annual servicing costs appear to be, instead of upfront capital costs, but the more expensive they will prove in real terms eventually. The OHE makes the point that, given that the taxpayer is going to pay in the end, there is no macroeconomic reason for preferring PFI to exchequer financing. The obvious missing format is public finance of the initial investment coupled with design, build and operate deals: this structure has not been attempted. The problem is that the Treasury effectively biases all comparisons by capping the public expenditure capital budget but imposing no limit on PFI-financed capital expenditure.

The problem of long-term large-scale project costing is well known in the defence industries. The established method of paying for defence supply contracts was to apply a cost-recovery formula after the event. If the contractor was deemed to have made excess profit, then the excess profit could and would be clawed back. Such provisions are strikingly absent from the PFI.

The combination of secrecy over figures, mismatching of risk and reward, and double payment for risk through the high discount rate, amply support the assertion that, so far as hospital building goes, PFI is indeed a thirty-year mortgage on the British economy, to be paid for by staffing cuts, longer waiting lists, early patient discharge, and the hidden costs of travel.

Now let's turn to schools. The method here is that the local education authority (LEA) buys a contract to design, build and operate a new school (as with hospitals, professional staff remain state employees). The Department for Education gives the LEA PFI credits to pay for the capital servicing element of the contract. School governors are required to accept the LEA's determination. Here we hit another problem, because official policy is that 'there is no alternative'. Any rational businessperson will cringe at such words. It is official policy that there must be a servicing element to each contract, i.e. maintenance and cleaning, which prevents simplification into the same 'design, build, operate' principle that the OHE noted was absent from hospitals. As with hospitals, concerns are being raised that PFI contract servicing will have priority over all other costs including teaching salaries, and therefore cuts in teaching staff may follow. It seems that there is no provision for fluctuating demand over the long period of these contracts, so changes in demographics leading to changes in school populations will result either in overcrowding or in overspending on excessive facilities at the inevitable expense of teaching.

As I browsed through various websites in which government departments, hospital trusts and LEAs uncritically praised their PFI projects, another thought struck me. There is a rash of building poorly designed schemes. There is no overall capital budget. Public-sector construction activity is at a high level. Eventually it must decline. How much of Britain's economic activity depends on this expansion of capital projects? What will happen when the PFI spending frenzy stops? Although the public imagination has not been captured, the whole process is reminiscent of something else we have seen in recent years: the rapid rise in activity, followed by the long decline as pay-up time comes round.

This is an unfashionable, and politically incorrect, point of view. Since we are all going to be paying for this bonanza, I feel perfectly entitled to state that it may not all be good value, even if it does pass the government's tests for value for money using artificially high discount rates. This approach took me to a report by the King's Fund, which argues that new hospitals are being built without regard to how they fit into the overall health service framework. Regional health authorities have been abolished. Primary and community services are not part of the usual hospital PFI project. New hospital capital projects worth £1.4 billion were agreed before the National Bed Inquiry reported. The government now says that the number of beds needs to increase and yet every PFI hospital project involves a reduction in beds. As we all know from recent experience, financial bubbles involve chucking money around in the vague hope it will do good, without thinking through all possible uses for the money.

Why is all this an accounting scandal? Well, we have the artificially high discount rate used to evaluate projects, apparent double compensation for risk, projects being authorised without considering the broader picture, unclear plans for balancing future budgets despite the extent to which they are committed, and the warning cry of "There is no alternative".

APPENDIX B: RIGHTS

The main rights are:

1. the right to life: suspicious deaths and deaths in custody must be investigated
2. the prohibition of torture and inhumane treatment
3. the right to protection against slavery and forced labour
4. the right to liberty and freedom
5. the right to a fair trial, and the right to be punished only in accordance with law, including the right to hear evidence against you in court
6. respect for privacy, family life, and the right to marry
7. the right to freedom of thought, religion and belief
8. the right to free speech and peaceful protest
9. the right to no discrimination by gender, race, sexuality, religion or age
10. the right to protection of property
11. the right to education

12. the right to free elections.

The right to seek asylum is enshrined in the refugee convention (1954). The United Kingdom has a habit of undermining basic rights. Examples are:

1. indefinite detention without trial (now abolished, but no doubt a future government will resurrect it)
2. restricting asylum applicants from working, limiting their benefits and delaying examination of claims, hence causing destitution and hardship (other countries place asylum seekers in suitable compulsory work)
3. extended immigration detention
4. the e-borders system, which enables government to retain extensive information on its citizens indefinitely
5. refusing legal aid to challenge immigration decisions
6. preventing some British citizens from bringing spouses and family to the United Kingdom.

The right to free speech has been undermined by using laws intended to curb antisocial behaviour, terrorism and serious crime, against protestors. In her book[104], Caroline Lucas describes how she was arrested for peacefully protesting against fracking and her resultant court victory over the police. Broadly drafted offences of encouragement and glorification of terrorism make careless talk a crime. Hate speech laws and stop and search powers have been expanded to the point that almost anything can be included. As for protesting, don't bother.

For a guide to how restricted free speech has become in the United Kingdom, here is part of the explanation from Wikipedia[105, 106]. Do you still understand your free speech rights after reading it?

APPENDIX B: RIGHTS

"...there is a broad sweep of exceptions including threatening, abusive or insulting words or behaviour intending or likely to cause harassment, alarm or distress or cause a breach of the peace (which has been used to prohibit racist speech targeted at individuals), sending any article which is indecent or grossly offensive with an intent to cause distress or anxiety (which has been used to prohibit speech of a racist or anti-religious nature), incitement, incitement to racial hatred, incitement to religious hatred, incitement to terrorism including encouragement of terrorism and dissemination of terrorist publications, glorifying terrorism, collection or possession of a document or record containing information likely to be of use to a terrorist, treason including advocating for the abolition of the monarchy or compassing or imagining the death of the monarch, sedition (no longer illegal, sedition and seditious libel (as common law offences) were abolished by section 73 of the Coroners and Justice Act 2009 (with effect on 12 January 2010)), obscenity, indecency including corruption of public morals and outraging public decency, defamation, prior restraint, restrictions on court reporting including names of victims and evidence and prejudicing or interfering with court proceedings, prohibition of post-trial interviews with jurors, scandalising the court by criticising or murmuring judges, time, manner, and place restrictions, harassment, privileged communications, trade secrets, classified material, copyright, patents, military conduct, and limitations on commercial speech such as advertising. So-called 'gagging orders' also serve as a form of censorship."

REFERENCES

Notes 24, 64, 71, 77, 82, 83, and 88 contain public sector information licensed under the Open Government Licence v3.0.

Notes 44, 48, 51, and 74 contain parliamentary information licensed under the Open Parliament Licence v3.0 https://www.parliament.uk/site-information/copyright-parliament/open-parliament-licence/

All references to theguardian.com are courtesy of *Guardian News & Media Ltd* and their Open Access licence.

All references to the *Financial Times* and ft.com are within the terms of their reproduction permission.

The opening poem was written by the former Children's Laureate in response to a government order to paint over murals in the children's section of the Kent asylum intake centre and is reproduced by permission of the author.
See https://twitter.com/MichaelRosenYes/status/1678008997201289217?s=20
and https://www.theguardian.com/commentisfree/2023/jul/11/

REFERENCES

robert-jenrick-mickey-mouse-anti-child-painting-over-mural-conservative-families by Polly Toynbee *accessed 11 July 2023*

1. Survey by Policy Institute at King's College London 30.3.23 https://www.kcl.ac.uk/news/uk-has-internationally-low-confidence-in-political-institutions-police-and-press *accessed 17 April 2023*

2. P Patel, R Swift and H Quilter-Pinner, 'Talking Politics: Building Support for Democratic Reform', IPPR https://www.ippr.org/research/publications/talking-politics-building-support-for-democratic-reform *accessed 27 June 2023*

3. Peter Oborne, *The Independent* daily edition, 8 May 2023, online at https://www.independent.co.uk/voices/king-charles-coronation-jeremy-corbyn-climate-b2334022.html *accessed 6 August 2023*

4. Camilla Cavendish, *Financial Times*, 13 January 2024, 'The UK has an accountability problem - just look at the Post Office', https://www.ft.com/content/12174950-8729-4ec0-95b0-693b76bce175

5. Dr Parth Patel, Institute for Public Policy Research, *The Guardian* 11 December 2023, https://www.theguardian.com/politics/2023/dec/11/next-uk-election-set-to-be-most-unequal-in-60-years-study-finds *accessed 24 January 2024*

6. Gavin Esler, *Britain is Better than This: Why a Great Country is Failing us All*, Apollo, 2023

7. Mark E Thomas. *99%: How We've Been Screwed and How to Fight Back*, Apollo, 2020

8. Rory Stewart, *Politics on the Edge*, Jonathan Cape, 2023

9. Suzanne Fitzpatrick, Glen Bramley, Morag Treanor, Janice Blenkinsopp, Jill McIntyre, Sarah Johnsen, and Lynne McMordie, 'Destitution in the UK 2023', https://www.jrf.org.uk/report-destitution-uk-2023 *accessed 26 October 2023*

REFERENCES

10. The new oil and gas licences are for sales outside the UK. They are needed to replace some of the government's revenue loss caused by Brexit. This appears to be an example of Brexit having an unintended environmental effect.

11. Jess Sargeant, Jack Pannell, Rebecca Mckee, Milo Hynes, Steph Coulter, https://www.instituteforgovernment.org.uk/publication/final-report-review-uk-constitution *accessed 26 October 2023*

12. Adam Posen, 'It is time for the UK to think like an emerging market', *Financial Times*, 24 June 2023, https://www.ft.com/content/4cf73b89-51eb-4144-a0e4-b6f08ecaee5

13. https://www.kingsfund.org.uk/publications/nhs-compare-health-care-systems-other-countries *accessed 26 June 2023*

14. Martin Wolf, *The Crisis of Democratic Capitalism*, Penguin, 2023

15. Jonty Bloom, 'Our go-it-alone government is becoming an international laughing stock', https://www.theneweuropeanco.uk/our-go-it-alone-government-is-becoming-an-international-laughing-stock/ *accessed 6 August 2023*

16. My data on rights has been taken from various sources including the European Convention on Human Rights and the European Union treaties.

17. Daniel Boffey, https://www.theguardian.com/technology/2023/dec/20/police-to-be-able-to-run-face-recognition-searches-on-50m-driving-licence-holders *accessed 20 December 2023*

18. https://www.conservatives.com/our-plan/conservative-party-manifesto-2019 *accessed 21 April 2023*

19. Jamal Osman, *The Guardian*, 26 May 2014, https:/wwwtheguardian.com/commentisfree/2014/may/26/british-citizen-passport-control *accessed 3 May 2023*

REFERENCES

20. https://www.youtube.com/watch?v=HTR9Pnsd0Sc *accessed 17 April 2023*.

    See also an article by Simon Kupfer, *Financial Times*, 28 October 2023

21. Mark Blyth, *Austerity: The History of a Dangerous Idea*, Oxford University Press, 2013

22. https://www.jrf.org.uk/report/brexit-vote-explained-poverty-low-skills-and-lack-opportunities *accessed 17 April 2023*

23. https://blogs.lse.ac.uk/politicsandpolicy/the-scrounger-myth-is-causing-real-suffering-to-many-in-society/ and https://en.wikipedia.org/wiki/Benefit_fraud_in_the_United_Kingdom (footnote 8) *both accessed 4 May 2023, see note 106 for attribution*

24. In 2021-20, 22 4.0% of total benefit expenditure was overpaid due to fraud and error, and the estimated value of overpayments was £8.6 billion. 1.2% of total benefit expenditure (or £2.6 billion) was underpaid due to fraud and error, and the net government loss, after recoveries, was £7.6 billion, or 3.5% of benefit expenditure https://www.gov.uk/government/statistics/fraud-and-error-in-the-benefit-system-financial-year-2021-to-2022-estimates *accessed 4 May 2023*

25. Patrick Butler, https://www.theguardian.com/business/2023/aug/18/uk-poorest-families-fall-in-living-standards *accessed 18 August 2023*

26. David Kauders, *Understanding Brexit Options: What Future for Britain?* Sparkling Books, 2016, ISBN 9781907230646

27. From 2004 to 2009, the UK was only on the losing side in 2.6% of European Council votes. That proportion increased after Cameron announced the referendum in 2013, since

REFERENCES

he wished to show that Britain was not a vassal state – by voting against measures that did not concern Britain.

See Simon Hix and Sara Hagemann, https://www.theguardian.com/world/datablog/2015/nov/02/is-uk-winner-or-loser-european-council *accessed 14 November 2023*

28. The EU works to prevent tax manipulation started with directive 2016/1164. There have been further changes since.

29. BBC *Question Time*, 2 March 2023, Sunderland

30. Simon Jenkins, https://www.theguardian.com/commentisfree/2023/jul/06/nhs-reform-royal-commission-politics *accessed 6 July 2023* and
Will Hutton, https://www.theguardian.com/commentisfree/2023/aug/13/uk-stop-kidding-ourselves-rich-nation-gone-bust *accessed 13 August 2023*

31. Multiple reports in UK press August 2023

32. https://www.taxresearch.org.uk/Blog/2022/08/29/we-could-massively-reduce-the-price-of-energy-in-the-uk-by-changing-the-way-we-regulate-energy-prices/ *accessed 18 April 2023*

33. https://www.taxresearch.org.uk/Blog/2022/03/12/oil-gas-and-energy-producer-profits-are-going-to-increase-40-fold-as-a-result-of-energy-price-increases/ *accessed 18 April 2023*

34. Jasper Jolly, https://www.theguardian.com/business/2022/aug/17/ofgem-director-christine-farnish-quits-over-energy-price-cap *accessed 8 December 2023*

35. https://www.independent.co.uk/news/business/energy-bills-rises-price-cap-b1981539.html *accessed 18 April 2023*

36. See as an example: Editorial, *The Observer*, https://wwwtheguardian.com/commentisfree/2022/aug/14/observer-view-woeful-state-uk-water-industry *accessed 18 April 2023*

REFERENCES

37. https://www.gmb.org.uk/news/more-70-englandswaterindustry-owned-foreign-companies *accessed 18 April 2023*. This may have changed subsequently.

38. Gill Plimmer, *Financial Times*, Macquarie 'transferred £2 bn of debt' on to Thames Water's books, 24 September 2017 *accessed 7 December 2023*

39. D Carey and J Morris, *King of Capital*, Crown Business, 2010

40. John Nelson, https://www.theguardian.com/business/2023jul/08/i-helped-privatise-uk-water-firms-but-its-government-inaction-that-wrecked-them *accessed 9 July 2023*

41. Brett Christophers, *Our Lives in Their Portfolios: Why Asset Managers Own the World*, Verso, 2023

42. Anna Isaac, https://www.theguardian.com/money/2023/aug/17/profits-soar-integrated-debt-services *accessed 17 August 2023*. One also wonders why the recently built car park that went up in flames at Luton airport on 10 October 2023 was not fitted with sprinklers.

43. https://youtu.be/gvagsSOlAy4 *accessed 18 April 2023*

44. https://committees.parliament.uk/committee/517/industry-and-regulators-committee/news/194330/failures-of-regulators-water-companies-and-government-leaving-public-and-environment-in-the-mire/ *accessed 18 April 2023*

45. Michael Goodier and Alexandra Topping, https://www.theguardian.com/business/2022/dec/26/great-britain-rail-system-dubbed-broken-as-years-data-reveals-extent-of-disruption *accessed 18 April 2023*

46. Hannah Devlin, https://www.theguardian.com/uk-news/2023/dec/21/surge-in-number-of-people-in-hospital-with-nutrient-deficiencies-nhs-figures-show *accessed 21 December 2023*

REFERENCES

47. Luca Calafati, Julie Froud, Colin Haslam, Sukhdev Johal and Karel Williams, *When Nothing Works: From Cost of Living to Foundational Liveability*, Manchester University Press, 2023

48. https://petition.parliament.uk/petitions/604892 *accessed 18 April 2023*

49. There have been at least three reports of expected losses from quantitative easing in the *Financial Times*: 25 July 2023, £150 bn; 21 December 2023, £126 bn., 26 March 2024 £100 bn. See
Delphine Strauss, 'UK government faces £150 bn bill to cover Bank of England's QE losses', 25 July 2023;
Chris Giles, 'BoE losses on QE greater than other central banks, says ex-rate setter', 21 December 2023; and
William Allen, 'Unwinding British QE may end up costing £100 bn. Could that have been avoided?', 26 March 2024

50. Ian Dunt, *How Westminster Works and Why it Doesn't*, Weidenfeld & Nicolson, 2023

51. From Prime Minister's Questions 6, June 2018: Mr Paul Sweeney (Glasgow North East) (Lab/Co-op):
Q10. "My constituent Giorgi is 10 years old. He was tragically orphaned in February. He has lived in Glasgow since he was three years old. His only language is English, and he speaks it with the same accent as mine. Yet he now faces being deported to Georgia, his late mother's country of birth, becoming another statistic who suffers at the hands of this prime minister's hostile environment policy. Will the prime minister promise today that Giorgi will not, under any circumstances, be torn from his school friends in Glasgow and sent to a country that is entirely foreign to him?"
The Prime Minister: "The honourable gentleman raises a very specific individual case. It is right that it be looked at properly, and that is what I will ask the Home Office to do."

REFERENCES

Hansard, Vol. 642, Col. 305, https://hansard.parliament.uk/commons/2018-06-06/debates/26753E92-D124-4BE2-A9DE-126B303829B3/Engagements *accessed 20 April 2023*

52. A qualified doctor who has passed her General Medical Council examinations was stuck in the UK asylum system for seven years. Miranda Bryant, https://www.theguardian.com/uk-news/2023/apr/09/trained-medics-who-could-ease-nhs-crisis-stuck-in-asylum-limbo *accessed 20 April 2023*

53. Multiple reports in *The Independent,* commencing 26 March 2023, see Holly Bancroft, https://www.independent.co.uk/news/uk/home-news/afghan-pilot-small-boat-deportation-rwanda-b2307456.html *accessed 26 March 2023*

54. Paul Johnson, *Follow the Money,* Abacus, 2023

55. Simon Jenkins, https://www.theguardian.com/commentisfree/2023/jul/14/rishi-sunak-public-sector-pay-rises-education-nhs *accessed 31 July 2023*

56. Kate Pickett and Richard Wilson, *The Spirit Level: Why Equality is Better for Everyone,* New Edition, Penguin, 2010

57. Michael Mansfield KC, *The Power in the People: How we Can Change the World,* Monoray, 2023

58. Hannah White, *Held in Contempt: What's Wrong with the House of Commons,* Manchester University Press, 2023

59. Linda Colley, 'Britain needs more than a streamlined coronation', *Financial Times,* 5 May 2023, see https://www.ft.com/content/c23bb75f-1f9b-4c3f-a8a4-5ceb5a670067

60. Heather Cox Richardson, *Democracy Awakening: Notes on the State of America,* Viking (USA), W H Allen (UK), 2023

61. Google searches 3 May 2023

REFERENCES

62. Jon Henley, https://www.theguardian.com/world/2019/apr/11/switzerland-court-overturns-referendum-as-voters-were-poorly-informed *accessed 8 December 2023*

63. Owen Jones, *The Establishment and How they Get Away with it*, Penguin, 2014; and
Nick Davies, *Flat Earth News*, Random House, 2008

64. https://www.ons.gov.uk/visualisations/dvc2205/fig2/data download.xlsx

65. See https://goodlawproject.org/ for an example

66. Anthony Seldon and Raymond Newell, *Johnson at 10: The Inside story*, Atlantic Books, 2023

67. David Kauders, *The Financial System Limit: The World's Real Debt Burden*, Sparkling Books, 2021, ISBN 9781907230790 (UK only), 9781907230769 (elsewhere)

68. Mary O'Hara, *Austerity Bites*, Policy Press, 2015;
Florian Schui, *Austerity: The Great Failure*, Yale University Press, 2015;
Kerry-Anne Mendoza, *Austerity: The Demolition of the Welfare State and the Rise of the Zombie Economy*, New Internationalist Publications, 2015;
Stewart Lansley and Joanna Mack, *Breadline Britain: The Rise of Mass Poverty*, Oneworld Publications, 2015; and
David Boyle, *Broke: How to Survive the Middle Class Crisis*, Harper Collins, 2014

69. https://www.un.org/dppa/decolonization/en/nsgt/gibraltar *accessed 21 April 2023*

70. https://www.gibraltarlaws.gov.gi/papers/gibraltar-constitution-order-2006-6# *accessed 28 November 2023* quoted by permission of the government of Gibraltar

REFERENCES

71. https://www.gov.uk/government/publications/highways-maintenance-funding-allocations/additional-budget-2023-highways-maintenance-and-pothole-repair-funding-2023-to-2024 *accessed 21 April 2023*

72. 'Begging bowl culture must end', *The Birmingham Mail,* https://www.birminghammail.co.uk/news/midlands-news/begging-bowl-culture-must-end-26020771 *accessed 21 April 2023*

73. The video clip of Rishi Sunak telling voters in Tunbridge Wells that he was diverting funds to them is at https://youtu.be/yKk3QQOsaTg *accessed 21 April 2023*

74. *Hansard,* volume 597, columns 186 ff, online at https://hansard.parliament.uk/Commons/2015-06-16/debates/15061658000001/EuropeanUnionReferendumBill *accessed 21 April 2023*

75. The Leave campaigns made contradictory promises as to whether Britain would leave everything or stay in the single market. Thus Daniel Hannan, 'Absolutely nobody is talking about threatening our place in the single market', 17 November 2016, see https://twitter.com/iandunt/status/799282286185222145
accessed 21 April 2023 (original tweet apparently removed)

76. 28 and 29 June 2023, see
https://www.youtube.com/watch?v=d1WNpYr96ec&embeds_referring_euri=https%3A%2F%2Fwww.ucl.ac.uk%2F&feature=emb_imp_woyt *observed 28 and 29 June 2023*

77. Northern Ireland Act 1998, Section 1

78. Simon Evans, *The Guardian,* https://www.theguardian.com/environment/2023/sep/29/how-a-thinktank-got-the-cost-of-net-zero-for-the-uk-wildly-wrong *accessed 27 October 2023*

79. https://search.electoralcommission.org.uk//Search/Accounts *accessed 4 May 2023*

REFERENCES

80. Other methods have been proposed in the past but, so far as I am aware, never implemented. The one coming closest to my proposal is to use the square root of population.

81. The facts hub has been proposed by Professor Alan Renwick, University College London Constitution Unit.

82. https://www.gov.uk/government/organisations *accessed 7 October 2023*

83. Constitutional Reform Act 2005 c. 4.

84. https://www.bbc.com/aboutthebbc/governance/charter *accessed 27 October 2023*

85. Consider the Financial Conduct Authority (FCA), which is a state-created monopoly regulator. It has legal powers exercised through its Regulatory Decisions Committee. This is a committee of the FCA board chaired by an FCA employee. Why is it not an independent court of law?

86. Alan Rusbridger, *The Independent* daily edition, 22 December 2023

87. Maurice Pope, *The Keys to Democracy: Sortition as a New Model for Citizen Power*, Imprint Academic, 2023

88. https://www.gov.uk/government/publications/professions-regulated-by-law-in-the-uk-and-their-regulators/uk-regulated-professions-and-their-regulators *accessed 30 April 2023*

89. RSA lecture, https://www.youtube.com/watch?v=gKAQcHaAAus *observed 26 October 2023*

90. 'UK in a changing Europe', https://www.youtube.com/watch?v=4TdsyCb1FXM *observed 20 September 2023*

91. Google searches 30 October 2023

92. https://www.gesetze-im-internet.deenglisch_gg/englisch_gg.html *accessed 9 June 2023*;

https://www.senato.it/documenti/repository/istituzione/costituzione_inglese.pdf *accessed 3 August 2023*; and https://www.fedlex.admin.ch/eli/cc/1999/404/en *accessed 9 June 2023*

93. For example, a former home secretary promised the Commons to see every asylum-seeker's file. The civil service simply wheeled a trolley of files past the home secretary's open office door. The files had been seen.

94. Federal Trust report 4 July 2022, see https://fedtrust.co.uk/getting-brexit-undone/; and lecture by Prof. A Blick, attended by this author

95. Anthony King, *The British Constitution*, (Chapter 7), Oxford University Press, 2007

96. Camilla Cavendish, 'The Whitehall Rolls-Royce desperately needs a service', *Financial Times*, 6 May 2023

97. "Sophie", https://www.theguardian.com/commentisfree/2023/jul/11/britain-benefits-system-universal-credit *accessed 11 July 2023*

98. The PFI data was researched from various sources in 2002. In 2010 the annual cost was revealed as £50 m. See https://www.scotsman.com/news/exclusive-well-pay-ps12bn-for-pfi-hospital-but-never-own-it-2442257 *accessed 18 April 2023*

99. Dr Richard Taylor served as an MP from 2001 to 2010.

100. In 2016, *the Eastern Daily Press* published a report on the dire financial outcome of this PFI, see https://www.edp24.co.uk/news/health/20859609.revealed-shareholders-pfi-firm-making-millions-cash-strapped-norfolk-norwich-university-hospital/ *accessed 18 April 2023*

REFERENCES

80. Other methods have been proposed in the past but, so far as I am aware, never implemented. The one coming closest to my proposal is to use the square root of population.

81. The facts hub has been proposed by Professor Alan Renwick, University College London Constitution Unit.

82. https://www.gov.uk/government/organisations *accessed 7 October 2023*

83. Constitutional Reform Act 2005 c. 4.

84. https://www.bbc.com/aboutthebbc/governance/charter *accessed 27 October 2023*

85. Consider the Financial Conduct Authority (FCA), which is a state-created monopoly regulator. It has legal powers exercised through its Regulatory Decisions Committee. This is a committee of the FCA board chaired by an FCA employee. Why is it not an independent court of law?

86. Alan Rusbridger, *The Independent* daily edition, 22 December 2023

87. Maurice Pope, *The Keys to Democracy: Sortition as a New Model for Citizen Power*, Imprint Academic, 2023

88. https://www.gov.uk/government/publications/professions-regulated-by-law-in-the-uk-and-their-regulators/uk-regulated-professions-and-their-regulators *accessed 30 April 2023*

89. RSA lecture, https://www.youtube.com/watch?v=gKAQcHaAAus *observed 26 October 2023*

90. 'UK in a changing Europe', https://www.youtube.com/watch?v=4TdsyCb1FXM *observed 20 September 2023*

91. Google searches 30 October 2023

92. https://www.gesetze-im-internet.deenglisch_gg/englisch_gg.html *accessed 9 June 2023*;

https://www.senato.it/documenti/repository/istituzione/costituzione_inglese.pdf *accessed 3 August 2023*; and https://www.fedlex.admin.ch/eli/cc/1999/404/en *accessed 9 June 2023*

93. For example, a former home secretary promised the Commons to see every asylum-seeker's file. The civil service simply wheeled a trolley of files past the home secretary's open office door. The files had been seen.

94. Federal Trust report 4 July 2022, see https://fedtrust.co.uk/getting-brexit-undone/; and lecture by Prof. A Blick, attended by this author

95. Anthony King, *The British Constitution*, (Chapter 7), Oxford University Press, 2007

96. Camilla Cavendish, 'The Whitehall Rolls-Royce desperately needs a service', *Financial Times*, 6 May 2023

97. "Sophie", https://www.theguardian.com/commentisfree/2023/jul/11/britain-benefits-system-universal-credit *accessed 11 July 2023*

98. The PFI data was researched from various sources in 2002. In 2010 the annual cost was revealed as £50 m. See https://www.scotsman.com/news/exclusive-well-pay-ps12bn-for-pfi-hospital-but-never-own-it-2442257 *accessed 18 April 2023*

99. Dr Richard Taylor served as an MP from 2001 to 2010.

100. In 2016, *the Eastern Daily Press* published a report on the dire financial outcome of this PFI, see https://www.edp24.co.uk/news/health/20859609.revealed-shareholders-pfi-firm-making-millions-cash-strapped-norfolk-norwich-university-hospital/ *accessed 18 April 2023*

REFERENCES

101. Felicity Lawrence, *The Guardian*, 23 July 2001, https://www.theguardian.com/society/2001/jul/23/hospitals *accessed 18 April 2023*

102. Sarah Boseley, *The Guardian*, 12 July 2001, https://www.theguardian.com/society/2001/jul/12/hospitals.privatefinance *accessed 18 April 2023*

103. https://www.ohe.org/publications/economics-private-finance-initiative-nhs/ *accessed 18 April 2023*

104. Caroline Lucas, *Honourable Friends: Parliament and the Fight for Change*, Granta, 2016

105. Wikipedia, https://en.wikipedia.org/wiki/Freedom_of_speech_by_country#United_Kingdom *accessed 3 May 2023*

106. Quoted under the terms of the Creative Commons Attribution-ShareAlike 3.0 Unported License (CC BY-SA) and, except where otherwise noted, the GNU Free Documentation License (GFDL)

INDEX

Figures and tables are indicated by an italic *f* or *t* following the page number. Notes in the References section are indicated by an italic *n* followed by the note number.

accounts
    government 156–8
    Treasury 109
    water companies 40–2
administrative secretariat (of People's Council) 186
Afghan Relocation and Assistance policy 52
AI *see* artificial intelligence (AI)
appointments 50, 51, 90–1, 125–6
artificial intelligence (AI) 82, 86–7, 135–6
"asset manager society" 43
asset prices 26, 69
Assize of Clarendon (1186) 29
asylum seekers 50, 52, 81–2, 134, 203, 205, 216*n*93
austerity 34, 36, 37, 38, 44, 69, 71–2
Australia 55, 57, 59*t*, 60, 61, 83, 112
autocracy
    government 25, 50–1, 67, 79, 91, 126, 169
    slide into 22–4, 28–9, 53, 115

backbenchers 49, 52, 115
Bank of England 50
banks 25–6, 50, 68, 72, 160–1
Barnett formula 61
BBC 35, 90
Belarus 29

Belfast Agreement (1998) 80, 117, 123, 167
benefits *see* social security benefits
Bennett Institute for Public Policy 76
Blair, Tony 33, 48, 119
Blick, Andrew 115
Blyth, Mark 68
borders 66–7, 86, 149, 203
borrowing 69, 108–9, 152, 156 *see also* debt
boundary changes 68, 147, 180
Brexit
    damage 22, 24, 37
    draining budgets 44
    and economic growth 80
    and failure of political governance 22
    and Gibraltar 70
    hard 48, 79, 148
    hidden costs 43, 207*n*10
    and instability 37
    and lack of truth 55
    as major policy failure 32, 34–6
    referendum 34–5, 76–8, 77*f*, 91
British Medical Journal 197
Brown, Gordon 23
Bucks and Oxon Union Bank 51
building industry 195
Bulb 40
business rates 108
businesses *see* companies

INDEX

by-laws 170

Cameron, David 76, 208*n*27
campaigns 80
Canada 35, 57, 59*t*, 60, 63, 112
capital gains taxes 108, 156-7
capital investment 47, 109, 152, 157
Carlisle 197
cash transfer mechanism 74, 75, 108, 112
Cavendish, Camilla 119
Cayman Islands 69, 83
CCTV 30
central banks 50, 68, 160-1
centralisation
    government 19, 46-8, 58, 59*t*, 61-2, 81, 111-12, 119
    media 46, 79
change
    case for constitutional 45-72
    to draft constitution 189-91
    how to achieve 114-20
    need for 106-7
charters 51, 151
China 23-4, 26
Christophers, Brett 43, 155
citizens
    alienation 58
    involvement 60, 67-8, 102
    juries 98
    and localism 112
    overseas territories 130
    put first 113, 129
    rights 29, 31, 65, 86-7, 130-8, 142-3
    and the State 136-8
civil penalties 29, 139-42, 173
civil service 50, 53, 56, 62, 119
'clear, fair, and not misleading' principle 20, 82-3, 91, 176, 178, 190
climate change 21, 31, 71, 72, 82
closed material proceedings 30
Colley, Linda 56
commercial penalties 140-2, 173
common standards 19, 159
communications 20, 82-3, 91, 124, 132, 167, 176-7
companies
    accounts 157
    compensation 184
    essential services 152-5
    liquidations 123
    and PFI 195
    rail 43-4
    regulation 159-60
    state-owned 145
    taxes 47, 108
    technology 86
    water 40-3, 92-3

compensation 72, 132-3, 154, 184
competition 59*t*, 62, 64, 65, 79, 81, 111, 160
complaints 93-4, 131-2, 170-1, 174-5
compromise 36, 48, 55, 65, 79
Conan Doyle, Arthur 25
Conservative Party 23, 30, 33
constitution
    achieving reform 114-18
    adopting the new 119
    amendments 180, 189-91
    case for change 45-72
    draft 77, 118-19, 121-93
    federal systems 57, 59*t*, 60, 73, 112-13
    Gibraltar 70
    need for 19, 20, 23, 25, 63, 67-8, 79, 106-7
    overseas territories 130
    and People's Council 88-9
    shortcomings of British 28-9, 51, 60, 67-8, 72, 76
    timeline for reform 120
    transitional provisions 191-2
Constitutional Court 89, 95, 193
consultations 46
Consumer Price Index 37
cooperation 62, 79, 81, 144-5
cooperative competition 81
Coroners and Justice Act (2009) 204
corruption 63, 87, 93
council taxes 108
courts 29-30, 51, 89, 95, 138-41, 193
Covid-19 pandemic 38, 113
credit crunch 25-6
credit expansion 26, 68-9
criminal matters 54, 93, 135, 139-41, 159, 175
criminal record checks 30
Crisis of Democratic Capitalism, The (Wolf) 24
Crown dependencies 69, 83, 130
Crown immunity 62-3, 65, 107, 180
Crown prerogative 60, 62-3, 65, 107, 126
Crown privilege 60, 107, 126
Crown prosecution service 139-40
culture 63, 150-1
Cumberland Royal Infirmary, Carlisle 197
currency 42-3, 152
customs and excise duties 108, 156
customs borders 66-7, 86
Cyprus 72, 130

databases 30
debt 24, 31, 50, 69, 71-2, 109, 156-7 *see also* borrowing
debt service costs 33, 68-9, 72, 108-9, 156
decline, British 21-4
defence 69-70, 81, 108, 149-50, 199
deflation 26, 195, 198

INDEX

democracy
    direct 60, 67-9, 73, 116-17
    and federalism 73-5, 116
    lack of 22-5, 46-53, 115-16
    principal concepts of reinventing 19-20
    solutions to reinvention 73-5
democratic deficit 28-9, 56
demonstration rights 30-1
Department for Education 199-200
derivatives 25-6, 40-2, 41t, 157
detention 140, 203
devolution 56, 59t, 62-5, 80, 87, 195-6
direct democracy 60, 67-9, 73, 116-17
'divine right of Kings' 20, 78
dot.com bust 25
draft constitution 77, 118-19, 121-93
Dunt, Ian 51, 52-3
Durham hospital 197, 197t

e-borders system 203
economic growth 24, 36, 38, 68, 80, 112
Edinburgh Royal Infirmary 196, 196t
education 53, 136-7, 150, 199-200
election manifestos 30, 49, 79, 96, 165-7
elections 79, 87, 100, 130-1, 163-8, 182-6
    general 30, 49, 66, 67, 79, 82
electoral system 22-3, 48, 56, 60, 62, 164-8
electricity generation 39
emergency services 149-50
emerging markets 22
employment 45, 137, 160
energy privatisation 39-40
England *see also* nations
    borders 66-7
    lack of parliament 64
    legislative mandates 95-6
    numerical dominance 20, 58, 61, 73, 76, 78, 83-4
    referendum for change 116-18
    responsibilities 106
    revenue 108
entry into force of draft constitution 188-9
equalisation funds 85, 145-7
Equality and Human Rights Commission (EHRC) 30
errors 93-4, 132-3, 141, 176
essential services 36, 45, 52-3, 151-5
Establishment 51, 61, 67, 80, 117, 118, 147
Europe
    borders 66-7, 86
    compromise 36
    relationship 28-9, 31, 115-16
    workers 71
European Convention on Human Rights (ECHR) 29, 50
European Council 34-5, 208n27
European Research Group 115

European Union (EU)
    borders 66-7
    customs union 116
    Dublin Regulation 82
    membership 28-9, 34-5, 55
    and Scotland 55, 66
    single market 86, 214n75
    tax directive 35, 209n28
European Union Referendum Bill 76
expenses 184
expertise 25, 102
extremism 26
extremist capture 22, 48, 51-2

facts hub 89, 94-5, 173
failure *see* policy failures
fair trial, right to a 29-30, 132, 202
Falconer, Lord 114, 115
farming 55, 116
Farnish, Christine 39
federal system of governance
    case for 71-2
    countries with 36, 57-62, 59t, 64, 112-13
    referendum on 116-18
    for the UK 19, 20, 56, 63-5, 67-8, 73-5, 78-81, 85, 106
Fibonacci series 83-4
Financial Conduct Authority (FCA) 44, 215n85
financial crisis (2007-2009) 25-6
financial engineering 25, 27, 33, 37-8, 43, 44, 154-5, 157-8
financial equalisation 85, 145-7
financial policies 68-9
financial regulation 27
Financial System Limit, The (Kauders) 68
Financial Times 33, 41
First Group 44
first-past-the-post electoral system 22-3, 48, 60
fixed-term parliaments 23
Follow the Money (Johnson) 53
foreign affairs 148-9
Foreign Office 69-70
France 26, 36
'free markets' 27
free movement rights 30-1, 47, 66
freedom of speech 58, 59t, 65, 132, 202, 203-4
freeports 55
free-trade agreements 27, 55
future forecasts 31

gas supply and distribution 21, 23, 39-40, 207n10
GDP *see* gross domestic product (GDP)
general elections 30, 49, 66, 67, 79, 82

INDEX

general group (of People's Council) 98, 99–100, 101f, 171–2, 181–3, 185–6
generations 75
    bias 31, 123
    older 31, 75
    younger 31, 69, 75, 97, 99, 100, 123
Germany 28, 36, 113
Gibraltar 69, 70, 76, 83, 90–1
gilts 50
governance
    federal systems 57–62
    levels 103–6, 104f, 105f
    need for change 106–7
    other changes 111–13
    pensions, healthcare costs, and social security 110–11
    revenue and borrowing 107–10
government
    accounts 156–8
    agencies 31, 92–3
    autocratic 25, 50–1, 79, 91, 126, 169
    centralisation 19, 46–8, 58, 59t, 61–2, 79, 81, 111–12, 119
    cooperation 144–5
    democratic deficit 56
    democratic deterioration 49–53
    elections 87
    federal systems 57–65, 59t
    lack of expertise 25
    legislation 23, 30, 95
    life-cycle 48–9
    new 103–13
    pensions, healthcare costs, and social security 110–11
    policy failures 52–5
    revenue and borrowing 107–10, 156
    senior minister qualifications 125–6
    separation from parliament 87
    sofa 48
gov.uk website 90
Greece 27
gross domestic product (GDP) 24, 38, 38t, 85
Guardian, The 197

Head of State 107, 124, 126
healthcare 22, 47–8, 64, 71, 111, 158, 200
Held in Contempt: What's Wrong with the House of Commons (White) 56
Home Office 52, 119
honours 74, 178, 187–8
Horizon Europe 78
hospitals 44, 194–200
House of Commons
    abolishment 95, 163–4
    and constitutional reform 114
    government control 23, 35, 49, 56, 78, 87, 89
    and legislation 74
    power 46
House of Lords
    lack of power 23, 46, 49, 51, 89, 95
    replacement 19, 73
House of Lords Appointments Commission 90–1
household debt 24, 50, 69
housing 161–2
How Westminster Works and Why it Doesn't (Dunt) 51, 52–3
HS2 high-speed railway 54
human rights 24, 29–31, 50, 202–4
Human Rights Act 29
hung parliaments 48, 115
Hungary 26
hypothecation 64

ideology 52–3
immigration 27, 47–8, 65, 203
income 36–7, 45, 54
income taxes 36–7, 108, 156
Independent, The 39
India 23
inequality 24, 54, 69, 85, 160
inflation 26
influence
    lack of 22, 24, 78, 79
    of oligarch class 33
    of organisations 90–1, 174
infrastructure 33, 86, 106, 151–5
inheritance taxes 110, 142
instability 36, 47
Institute for Government 76
Institute for Public Policy Research 198
Integrated Care Boards 128–9, 146
international agreements 86, 96–7, 106, 178–9, 191
Iran 23–4
Isle of Man 69, 83
Italy 43, 76, 113

Jenkins, Simon 35
Jersey 69, 70, 83
Johnson, Paul 53
Judicial Appointments Commission 90–1
Judicial Committee 51
Justice and Security Act (2013) 30

Kidderminster 196–7
King, Anthony 119
King's Fund 22, 195, 200
King's speech 56

Labour Party 33
language 59t, 63, 63t, 132, 134
law 138–43, 168–70 *see also* legislation

INDEX

leadership 100, 112, 183, 184–5
Leave campaigns 35, 214*n*75
Leeds University 195
legislation
    arbiter 88, 173
    assent 94, 96–7
    in draft constitution 168–70
    and government 23
    and House of Lords 51
    mandates and venues 95–7
    one-off 64
    and Privy Council 51
    shortcomings 44
Liberal Democrats 23
Lidington, David 76, 79
lies
    and Brexit referendum 22, 34–5, 91
    political 28, 33–4
listening to the people 93–4
living standards 34, 37, 37–8, 38*t*, 84–5, 85
Lloyd George, David 23, 46
Lloyds Bank 51
lobbying 20, 63, 143
local authorities
    and centralisation 62
    elections 163–4
    and equalisation 85, 145–7
    governance responsibilities 104*f*, 105*f*
    and infrastructure planning 151
    larger 46
    and ombudspersons 170–1
    and regional government 128
    and surveillance 30
local control 75, 80–1, 84–5, 93, 112, 118
local education authorities (LEAs) 199–200
local government
    and centralisation 58
    and civil service 119
    and leadership 112
    and local control 81
    and revenue 84, 108
local taxes 108
Lucas, Caroline 203

Macquarie 41–2
Magna Carta (1215) 29
Major, John 33
Manchester 189
manifestos 30, 49, 79, 96, 165–7
Mansfield, Michael 54–5
'matrix management' 80–1
May, Theresa 48
mayors 80, 112
media
    behaviour 175
    centralisation 46, 79
    control 21
    mass 48
    truthfulness and standards 91–2, 176–7
medical professionals 71
middle classes 36, 69
military 24, 69, 149–50
ministers 25, 53, 125–6
minorities 48–9
minority capture 49, 78
misinformation 82–3, 91
misrepresentations *see* lies
monarchy 70, 107, 124, 126
Monbiot, George 33
monetary policy 160–1
multiculturalism 63
Murphy, Richard 39

National Bed Inquiry 200
national debt 109, 156–7
National Health Service *see* NHS
nationalisations 155
nations
    borders 66–7
    citizens 130–1
    culture, education and religion 150–1
    devolution 62–5
    in draft constitution 121–93
    and federalism 73–5
    governance responsibilities 104*f*, 105*f*, 106
    international agreements 86
    principal concepts 19–20
    referenda 68, 116–17
    revenue 84–5, 108
    social objectives 144
    sovereignty 19, 77–8, 80–1
    taxes 110, 156–7
naturalisations 134–5
neglect 35, 44, 52
neo-liberalism 33, 68–9, 71–2
net zero targets 31, 72
newspapers *see* media
NHS 37, 71, 115, 196
North Korea 23
Northern Ireland
    Belfast Agreement (1998) 80, 117, 123, 167
    and Brexit referendum 76, 78
    and international agreements 86, 106
    language 63
    referendum for change 117
Norwich 197

Office for National Statistics (ONS) 37, 85
Office of Gas and Electricity Markets (OFGEM) 39–40, 44
Office of Health Economics (OHE) 195, 198, 199

INDEX

OFGEM *see* Office of Gas and Electricity Markets (OFGEM)
OFWAT *see* Water Services Regulation Authority (OFWAT)
OHE *see* Office of Health Economics (OHE)
oil and gas 21, 23, 207*n*10
older generations 31, 75
oligarch class 33, 35, 36
ombudspersons 89, 94, 170-1
ONS *see* Office for National Statistics (ONS)
oppositions 48, 49
Orders in Council 62-3, 70, 91
organisations 90-1, 145, 160, 173-5
Osman, Jamal 31
overseas territories 19, 69-70, 83, 108, 130, 192
oversight 103-6

parliamentary petitions 46-7
parliaments
    and Brexit referendum 76-7
    elections 87, 163-4
    equal powers 46
    extremist capture 48
    government control 35
    hung 48, 115
    and legislation 23, 168-9
    legislative mandates and venues 95-6, 107, 127-8, 129
    minority capture 49
    need for reform 56
    separation from government 87
    sovereignty 77-8
part-time involvement 19, 31, 74-5, 100, 112, 184
party coalitions 23, 36
party whips 35, 51, 56, 76, 89, 96
passports 131, 133, 134
patronage 114
penalties 29, 139-42, 173
pensions 110-11, 162
People's Assent 68, 96-7, 178-9
People's Council
    choosing and refreshing 97-102, 101*f*
    and Constitutional Court 193
    in draft constitution 171-87
    functions 88-95
    legislative mandates and venues 95-7
    membership 181-7
    as principal concept 19
Peston, Robert 102
Pitcairn 69
Plaid Cymru 56
police 30, 149-50
policy failures 21, 32-43, 53-4
political advisers 53, 97, 126
political discourse 50, 53, 102

political evolution, dead-end of 46-53
political parties 82, 165
political upsets 26-7
politicians
    behaviour 21, 50, 52
    distrust of 55, 56
    and future trends 31
    misleading 34, 80
population 38, 38*t*, 58, 69, 73, 83
Posen, Dr Adam 22, 33
pothole fund 75, 85
Power in the People, The (Mansfield) 54-5
prime ministers 56, 64, 74, 79, 114
Prime Minister's Questions 52
principal concepts (of reinventing democracy) 19-20
Prison Officers Association 194
prisons 35, 194
privacy 24, 30
private finance initiative (PFI) 33, 37, 38, 44, 46, 194-201, 216*n*98
privatisation 32-3, 39-44, 46, 53
Privy Council 19, 51, 65, 70, 102, 107, 187
probation service 53
professions 99, 100, 101*f*, 159, 172, 181
proportional representation (PR) 49, 51-2
public appointments *see* appointments
public expenditure 59*t*, 61-2, 109, 194-201
public funding 84-5, 108-10
public life 91, 136
public services 33, 34, 36, 37, 71, 111

qualifications 125-6
quantitative easing (QE) 38, 50, 54, 69, 211*n*49
Question Time (TV programme) 35

railways 33, 43-4, 54
random selection 98
recession 25-6
referenda
    Brexit 34-5, 76-8, 77*f*, 91
    on constitutional reform 116-18, 188-9
    in draft constitution 164-7, 177-80
    in federal systems 60, 64
    and local authorities 170
    and majority vote 20
    requests 93
    in UK 67-8
refugees 27, 65, 134
regional governments
    in draft constitution 121-93
    and federalism 74-5, 79, 80-1, 85, 106, 112
    governance responsibilities 104*f*, 106
    and local initiative 118
    revenue source 108

INDEX

religion 151
rent extraction 33, 38, 155, 157-8
Retail Price Index (RPI) 37, 38*t*
Richardson, Heather Cox 57
right to a fair trial 29-30, 132, 202
rights *see* human rights
Rowntree Foundation 34
royal assent 51, 68, 94, 95, 168
Royal Commissions 35
Royal palaces 107
RPI *see* Retail Price Index (RPI)
Russia 23, 29
Rwanda 50

Salisbury convention 49
Saudi Arabia 24
Schengen area 34-5, 66-7
schools 35, 44, 199-200
Scotland *see also* nations
    borders 66-7
    and Brexit referendum 76, 78
    devolution 62-5
    independence 56, 72
    language 63
    PFI projects 195-6
    referendum for change 117
Scottish National Party (SNP) 27, 56, 62, 66
security 149-50
self-incrimination 58, 59*t*
senior ministers 125-6
serfdom 20, 25, 49-50
Severn Trent Water 42
short-termism 47, 53, 71
Sign of the Four, The (Conan Doyle) 25
Smith, Adam 27
SNP *see* Scottish National Party (SNP)
social care 37, 48
social media 83
social objectives 144
social security benefits 34, 111, 146, 162, 208*n*24
society, success of 45-6
soft power 50, 90
sortition group 100, 101*f*, 185-6
South Africa 23
sovereignty 19, 77-8, 81-2, 111-12
Spain 70
Special Immigration Appeals Commission 30
State
    and citizens 136-8
    in draft constitution 121-93
    organisations forming 90-1
    and People's Council 91, 173-4
    power 113
    principal concepts 20
Supreme Court 51, 138, 139, 193

surveillance powers 30-1
Switzerland
    compromise 36
    constitution 113, 122
    and the EU 55, 66
    federalism 57, 59*t*, 61, 64, 72, 83
    rail fares 43
    referenda 60, 76

tax havens 70
taxation policy 36-7, 47, 61
taxes
    allocation 64
    capital gains 108, 156-7
    company 47, 108
    cuts 34, 36
    income 36-7, 108, 156
    inheritance 110, 142
    local 108
    nations 110, 156-7
    and oligarch class 33
    and QE losses 50
    regional governments 157
    for revenue 107-8
    value added (VAT) 108, 156
    wealth 33, 110, 156-7
    withholding 108, 156
Taylor, Dr Richard 216*n*99
technology industries 86-7, 155
telecommunications 33
Thames Water 40-2, 41*t*
trade agreements 35, 55, 86, 116, 148, 178, 191
transitional arrangements 191-2
transport 36, 64
Treasury 50, 64, 109, 119, 199
Treasury accounts 109
trend forecasts 31
truth 24-7, 54-5, 91-3
TSSA rail union 44
Turkey 67
two parties system 21, 47, 56, 60, 67, 80, 118

unions, public sector 195
United Kingdom (UK)
    draft constitution 121-93
    governance responsibilities 104*f*, 105*f*
    government revenue and borrowing 107-10
    public sector 103-6
United States of America
    Bill of Rights 57, 72
    extremism 26
    federalism 57, 59*t*, 72, 83
    population 58
    referenda 60

INDEX

separation of governments and parliament 87
Universal Declaration of Human Rights (1948) 29
universities 53, 150
user fees 110
utilities *see* essential services

value added tax (VAT) 108, 156
voting rights 30-1, 46, 82, 165
vouchers (for political party funding) 82, 168

Wales *see also* nations
  borders 66
  and Brexit referendum 76, 78
  devolution 62-5
  language 63
  referendum for change 117
  water 40
water privatisation 33, 35, 40-3, 44, 92-3

Water Services Regulation Authority (OFWAT) 40, 44
wealth inequality 54
Wealth of Nations, The (Smith) 27
wealth taxes 33, 110, 156-7
Westminster, palace of 95-6, 107, 127-8
Westminster Hall 95, 127
When Nothing Works (Calafati, Froud, Haslam, Johal and Williams) 45
White, Hannah 56
withholding taxes 108, 156
Wolf, Martin 24
women's emancipation 80, 114
work visas 110
World Trade Organisation 86

Yorkshire Water 42
younger generation 31, 69, 75, 97, 99, 100, 123

For details of all Sparkling Books please visit
www.sparklingbooks.com